TALKING FOOTBALL
(HALL OF FAMERS' REMEMBRANCES)
VOLUME 4

AUTHOR: DAVID SPADA

EDITED BY MELINDA SPADA

TALKING FOOTBALL
(HALL OF FAMERS' REMEMBRANCES)
VOLUME 4

ISBN: 978-0-692-07880-8

Printed in USA

Table of Contents

About the Author 1

Chapter 1 Jerry Kramer 2

Chapter 2 Bobby Beathard 14

Chapter 3 Jimmy Johnson 22

Chapter 4 Mel Blount 28

Chapter 5 Robert Brazile 34

Chapter 6 Kellen Winslow 40

Chapter 7 Kenny Easley 48

Chapter 8 Russ Grimm 56

Chapter 9 Mike Munchak 62

Chapter 10 Morten Anderson 74

Chapter 11 Bruce Matthews 80

Chapter 12 Terrell Davis 86

ABOUT THE AUTHOR

David Spada is a successful attorney whose dream was to become a sports talk show host. David teamed up with Elliott Harris in 2011 to host the sports podcast "Sports & Torts" on talkzone.com. "Sports & Torts" was a finalist for Sports Podcast Of the Year in 2013 by the website podcastawards.com. David has interviewed over 210 Hall of Famers from the world of football, baseball, and basketball. David is pleased by share his interviews with 12 Pro Football Hall Of Famers who talk about their careers in this book.

Chapter 1

Jerry Kramer

College: Idaho
Career History: Green Bay Packers (1958-1968)
2018 Inductee Pro Football Hall Of Fame

College Choice

I had a chance to go to Washington State, University of Washington, and a couple other schools. My dad had a business in Sandpoint, Idaho, and some of the business people were encouraging him to have me go to the University of Idaho.

I was visiting University of Washington and the coach took me out on the field and introduced me to the team in the middle of a scrimmage. He also took me to dinner. He had a boat and wanted to take me fishing up the West Coast and into Canada. He said they'd fly my folks to every home game for three years. So, I called my dad and told him the offer.

My dad said, "I don't need to fly to a home game. I need to go to a game I can drive to. You get home. You're going to Idaho."

I start thinking about it and realized that if I went to Idaho, I'd probably play a lot. The better I play, the better I'll get, and the more I play, the better I'll get. Idaho played Oregon, Oregon State, Washington, and Washington State at that time, so it was a pretty good schedule. They were competing against some really good schools, so I decided I would go to Idaho and keep peace in the family, in the little town of Sandpoint.

College

Idaho was fantasyland for me. Going to college was not on my radar through high school and all of a sudden it jumped up in the form of scholarships. No one had gone to college amongst my six brothers and sisters. My older brother had gotten married and went to work. My older sister got married. So it was quite an experience for me.

I joined a fraternity and became a Sigma Nu. That was another part of college that was unknown to me. I was a wonderful experience. I had a great time in college. I just loved it. I had great pals, both on the football team and in the fraternity. So many became lifelong pals. Everybody was young, optimistic, and full of fun. It was a wonderful time.

I really enjoyed college. The games were kind of long and arduous. We would average 59 minutes a game. We would be out for five or six minutes the last game of the season and that would make it 59 minutes because we played damn near every snap both ways. We had three or four other kids that played professional football. Wayne Walker, Tony Anderson, and Jim Prestel played in the NFL. Bobby Dillinger played in Canada. Jim Norton played in Houston in the American Football League [at that time]. So, there were some pretty good players but just not very many of them on the team.

College All-Star Game

I played in the Senior Bowl. Wayne Walker and I played in the East-West Shrine Game and the College All-Star Game. That was really a wonderful step between college football and professional football because kids from Ohio State, Notre Dame, Michigan, West Virginia, and from all over the country were on our team and as opponents on the field. So it was a huge thing for us, maybe one of the bigger things in our lives up to that point. Otto Graham was our coach at the College All-Star game and John Sandusky was my line coach.

Playing in the College All-Star Game was a huge thrill. We beat the Detroit Lions and put them on the skids for 50 or 60 years, whatever it's been now. My pal Wayne Walker never got over it. He really had a hard time with my success and his lack of success. He thought I was lucky, and I was.

The College All-Star Game was a big start for me. If you can play against those guys in the game, and those are the kind of guys that are going into the league, you can probably play in the league. It was a defining moment for us in terms of our confidence.

John David Crow, Jin Ninowski, Jim Taylor, and Joe Nicely from West Virginia, and Dan Currie, Bobby Mitchell, and Charlie Krueger from Texas A&M were on the college team. Charlie Krueger was about three days late getting into training camp for the game.

Charlie's wife would call every 15 minutes and say, "Is Charles Kruger by y'all?" I'd answer, "No, ma'am. Charlie is not here." She was calling literally day and night, until he arrived. For the rest of the camp we were all messing with him, "Is Charles Kruger there?"

I wrote about this in Instant Replay during the 1967 season. In 1968, we were playing the San Francisco 49ers in Green Bay and Charlie was playing defensive tackle against me. I went into this mental thing to prepare for a game. I got angry and generated a manageable intelligent anger that got my juices flowing. It was kind of like, I'll show that son of a ... It kind of helped me get ready to play. I didn't want to talk to anybody, didn't want to look at anybody, and didn't want to have any conversations. I just wanted to work on my mind and my emotions. I was out on the field and was going through all of this. I didn't look at anybody. I finished my warm-ups and I went back into the locker room for the last two or three minutes of pregame conversation. I was going up the steps and I felt this presence right behind me, almost brushing me. The voice leaned up against my ear and said, "Is Gerald Kramer there?"

I said, "God damn you, Charlie. You just destroyed me." He knew it too. He read Instant Replay and knew what I was doing and what I was thinking, and he just destroyed my preparation. I enjoyed the hell out of him and John David and all the guys. It was just a fun, fun time.

Wayne Walker

Wayne Walker and I drove to the College All-Star Game together. I had a little Chevy convertible with baby blue seats and top. We gave ourselves ten days to get ourselves from Boise, Idaho to Chicago, Illinois. Seven days out we're in West Yellowstone. So we had to kick it in gear. All the way back from Chicago Wayne is saying, "I'm going to play for the World Champion Detroit Lions with Joe Schmidt, Roger Zatkoff, Jim Martin, and Bobby Layne, and you're going to Green Bay." He busted my ass all the way from Boise to Chicago with that noise. He was tickled to death to be going to Detroit.

I had gotten a little more publicity than Wayne in college. Wayne played as much as I did and he was a hell of a football player. He had a wonderful career, but he kept comparing his career to mine. In the NFL I won championships and Wayne didn't, so he was always a little feisty with me. He was a little fussy about Green Bay; he had a difficult time with it. It worked out just fine for me, but Wayne had a problem with it.

John Sandusky

I had an interesting deal with John Sandusky. He told me that I wasn't going to make the Green Bay Packers. He said, "You'll be able to play, but you just won't make the Green Bay Packer team." I looked at him kind of funny. He said, "They got five veteran guards returning." So, I'm going well okay. I go to Green Bay. Scooter McLean is our head coach and he calls me into his office and says, "What in the hell is wrong with you?" I said, "What do you mean, coach?" Well you're looking out in the crowd, you're giggling, you're playing grab ass, you're not watching the scrimmage; you just don't seem to be engaged. I said, "Well, I'm waiting to be traded." He said "You're what?" I said, "My college All-Star coach told me I'd be traded. He said I wouldn't make this team, so I'm waiting to be traded." Coach McLean said, "Well I didn't draft you to trade you. You're starting Friday night." So that gave me a couple of days to think about what he said.

It was an interesting final cut. We were down to 37 guys on the club and we were going to keep 36. There was another guard named Kenny Gray, who later played with the Cardinals. It came down to one of us would make the team. Kenny had been there the whole camp. He was playing defensive tackle and making himself valuable. He was a good football player and a good guard. I saw him the day that I got the news that I was going to make the team and be a Green Bay Packer. I'm down at the cigar store, picking up some magazines and he's across the street from the store when I come out. He hollers across the street, "Son of a bitch, you had a no cut contract, didn't you?" I go, "What's a no cut contract?"

After he was released, he went to St. Louis and played for ten or twelve years. He wore the number 64 down there. He was a good football player, and I believe he was an All-Pro at some point.

Detroit Lions

The whole Detroit team has a problem with the Packers. We beat the Lions in Green Bay, 9-7, in Lombardi's first or second year coaching Green Bay on a field goal winning kick. Our kicker kicked it like 50 yards, unobstructed, and we won the game in the last few seconds. The Lions' quarterback, Milt Plum, had thrown an interception. The Lions' players were just going crazy in the locker room. They're throwing garbage cans around, breaking shit, and just going nuts. The Lions thought they had us beat during the game.

We went to the playoffs six or seven times and the Lions didn't. They were in the same division as us. They had good reason to be angry with us.

Vince Lombardi

Everything changed when the Green Bay Packers hired Vince Lombardi as Head Coach. The Packers players were having fun before Coach Lombardi arrived. We were just tickled to death to be professional football players. We were drinking beer, hanging out, bullshitting, and just enjoying every aspect of being professional football players. We did very little conditioning. Our conditioning consisted of waving our arms and making our fingers go up and down.

Scooter McLean, our head coach, would play gin with Paul Hornung, Max McGee, and one of the other guys. In 1958, we were 1-10-1. After about the fourth loss or so, it got so painful to go downtown that

4

we started staying in the locker room to have our celebrations.

Players would take their babies and go home, check everything out, and get the baby sitters stabilized. We would come back to the locker room with our wives and bring a bottle. We had a coke machine, an ice machine, and a juke box in the locker room. There must have been 20-25 couples. We'd kick the socks and jocks out of the way and dance; have a party and have a few drinks. We weren't going downtown, but we were still having a hell of a good time. Local folks in Green Bay wanted to know what the hell was going on.

Coach Lombardi laid it out in his first meeting. He said, "I've never been a loser and I'm not about to start now. If you're not willing to make the sacrifice to pay the price to support your team and do the things you need to do to win, then get the hell out. The three things in your life should be your God, your family, and the Green Bay Packers. That's it. We're going to work harder than we have ever worked before. There are planes and trains and buses leaving here every day. I have a five year contract and some of you may be on the team."

He laid out the kind of work we were getting into pretty clearly. We didn't believe him until we got on the field and people started losing consciousness. We would just kneel over them, throw water on them, move them off to the side, and keep on going.

After one practice Leon Crenshaw showered, got on the bus, and went back to Saint Norbert. While he was standing in the cafeteria line, he lost consciousness and crumpled over.

There was a scout from the St. Louis Cardinals on the sidelines by the tower one day. I came out of the scrimmage and he looked at me and said, "Jerry, I have never seen anything like this. I have never seen anybody work like how you guys are working." He said, "If we did this in St. Louis half of the guys would quit and the other half would be dead."

It was extreme conditioning. You knew that the spark in Lombardi was what really made the difference.

Prior to Coach Lombardi we had good football players who were fast, and had all the qualifications and characteristics necessary to play the game. We didn't have a fire, a burn, a direction, or a spark in us. Coach Lombardi put that spark, that fire, and that drive in you. He said he coached 40 individual people, not a team of 40 people.

Coach Lombardi told me, after chewing me out unmercifully, that I was going to be one of the best guards in football. Herb Adderley came off the field one day and Coach Lombardi ran up to Herb and said, "Herbie, you have just played the finest game I have ever seen a cornerback play. You take that with you whenever you walk on the field in the future.

Carry that thought with you." Herbie said, "For the rest of my career, whenever I walked on the field, guess what I remembered." Coach Lombardi found out when and where you were most vulnerable and he would either pat you on the back, chew your ass, or both.

The one thing that was really consistent and interesting about him is he never left a practice without re-establishing communications. He chewed me out for jumping offsides. He came in the locker room looking for me. He patted me on the shoulders and re-established communications.

That was part of the brilliance of him. You'd know, okay he chewed me out, but I made a mistake. Maybe I should have been chewed out. I'll be a little more focused next time and maybe I won't make

the mistake. If he thinks I can be really good, maybe I can, maybe I can be something special. So he was the magic of it all. It was the emotional package that he brought that he created in each and every one of us that made the difference.

Green Bay Packers Only Losing One Playoff Game Entire Time Vince Lombardi Was Head Coach
This will not happen again not under the current rules. The NFL looks for competitive balance today with the salary cap, the ability of players to move from team to team, and with so many of the rules today made to create an even field for everybody. Obviously today there are eight to ten teams that seem to be in the mix all the time.

A team can't keep an offensive line together for ten years. A team has to pay players too much and doesn't have enough money to pay all their offensive linemen if they are going to pay the quarterback what he deserves or what he can get as a free agent. The eight-year veteran is as expensive as hell and a team can't afford him, so it's more difficult today to build a dynasty.

Last Drive Of "Ice Bowl" Dallas Cowboys vs. Green Bay Packers
We've heard or read of a lady being able to lift a car off of a baby—that is like the Green Bay Packers last drive in the "Ice Bowl". We [Green Bay Packers] got the ball with four and a half minutes to go. We were on the 35-yard line. We had 65 yards left to go to score. It was minus 57°outside and we were freezing our asses. We made a minus nine yards in our previous 31 plays.

Bart Starr got in the huddle and said, "Alright, let's go." That's all he said. The generation of emotion, the drive, the hunger, the want, the burn, the fire, whatever the hell you want to call it, kicked in and everybody on that team felt it and made a contribution. We went down the field to score and win with 13 seconds to go. You can get a guy with legs, you can get a guy with size, and you can get a guy with speed, but give me a guy with heart.

Ron Kostelnik
Ron Kostelnik joined us during my third or fourth year with the Green Bay Packers. Ron had a little bit of a dunlop coming over his belt and he was not well defined. He looked chubby, rather than muscular. I looked at him and said, "Boy, this kid is not going to be here long." Well he started nine years for us. They couldn't measure his heart, his want, or his fire.

Why Played Injured
I played with broken ribs for the team not for the money, not for the coach, but for the guys. I played with a 103° fever, a busted thumb, concussions, detached retinas … all kinds of shit. But, I didn't play for the coach; I played for the guys.

Bart Starr
There was a single moment in Bart Starr's career that changed our opinion of him, and I believe it changed his life. We were playing the Bears. The nasty Bears with their nasty middle linebacker Bill George. Our coach told Bart to throw the ball deep. He would throw it underneath, and the safeties were coming up threatening to intercept Bart. Our coach said, "Just throw the damn thing as far as you can throw it. I don't care if you complete it or not, just throw it down the field."

So we've got a pass play and Bart goes back to throw and throws the ball. Our tackle stops and turns around and watches the ball. Bart and I are also watching the ball. Bill George is not watching the ball. Bill takes about a five-yard run and hits Bart with a forearm, right square in the mouth and

knocks him backward about five yards. Bill says to Bart, "That ought to take care of you Starr." Bart Starr responded, "F— you, Bill George. We're coming after you."

Bart's upper lip was split all the way up into his nose. Blood is flowing down the front of his jersey. I said, "Bart, you better go to the sidelines to get sewed up." He said, "Shut up and get in the huddle." I said, "Yes sir. Yes sir, Mr. Starr."

Bart took us down the field in eight or nine plays for a score. Then he went to the sidelines like the rest of us and they laid him down on the bench. We weren't as delicate as these young boys today. They put about 11 stitches in Bart's upper lip and he went back into the game the next time we got the ball. He never missed a play.

The only question really about Bart up to that point was his toughness, was he tough enough to play. That game answered that question very loudly and very completely. For the rest of Bart's career I never doubted Bart Starr. He became our leader.

Many times I thought I had a play that might work and I'd talk to Bart about it. One time Bart said, "Well Jerry, talk to the other guys, see what they have to say. Do they think it will work?" So from that point on, I would go to either Jim Ringo, Ken Bowman, Fuzzy Thurston, Forrest Gregg, Bob Skoronski, Bill Curry, or whoever the hell was in the game and I'd say, "It looks to me like this play would work for us. It looks good from my standpoint, what do you think?" They would say, "Yeah, Jerry. I think it will work. Yeah, yeah, yeah."

Then I would go to Bart and I'd say, "Everybody thinks it will work, so if you need it, this play is available." Bart showed that fire and he was bright. He did things I don't think people often do.

We were playing the Bears again. We had a cadence where when we would get to the line of scrimmage, it was a set, a single digit number and a double digit number and a series of huts, as in, two, 48, hut, hut, hut. Bart had said that if the quarterback repeats the snap count, say it's on two and he comes up to the line of scrimmage and he says, "Two," then it's a brand new play and the next double digit number is the play, and it goes on the second hut.

So we call this play on one and Bart comes up to the line of scrimmage and breaks the huddle. He comes up to the line of scrimmage and he says, "Set, two, 46," and the whole Bear defense moves shifting over to our right (their left). The Bears were going to kill our play. They were going to overwhelm our play. We had no shot. The next thing I hear is "hut." Bart called it on one actually. Bart came up and said, "Two 47." So it's supposed to go on the first hut and the play is dead, dead, dead.

I'm thinking, "Jesus, I got this. Unless I hear a hut, I've got to block this 280 pound idiot across the line of scrimmage from me or Bart if changes it, I may have to pull left."

It's bad to be in that state. It's tough to anticipate, tough to get a good start, and tough to do everything. Bart said, "Easy, hold it, one 36, hut." There wasn't a missed assignment; there wasn't a single guy that was out of focus. We were waiting on Bart to change the play and Bart knew that. Bart knew his game and he knew our game. He was just a bright, intelligent, human being and was tough as nails. Zeke Bratkowski said one time, "You may think Bart's a sweetheart, but he'll cut your heart out if he has to."

Jim Taylor Leading the NFL In Rushing Being Only Time In Jim Brown's Career Jim Didn't
The Green Bay Packers really were a team. We wanted the team to win and individual accomplishments weren't made out to be that big of a deal.

We would have a game against the Cleveland Browns and everybody knew that Jim Brown was having a war with Jim Taylor and Taylor was having a war with Brown. So we may have given a little more, but we didn't have a lot extra to give. We were playing with everything we had. We were happy when Jimmy came out ahead. We thought that reflected on us and we were proud.

Jim Taylor & Paul Hornung
There was always a feeling our running game was pretty much our bread and butter, so we were running most of the time. Passes were mixed in to confuse our opponent.

Jim Taylor and Paul Hornung were different types of runners. Jimmy was more brutal; a brute force. Hornung was more cerebral. Hornung would see a defensive back and he would know that I had to block the defensive back. He would be under enough control to get at the magic point when the defensive back had to make a decision, and if he didn't, I was going to kill the defensive back. Hornung would be in a position where he had to move. At that instant, he would take a step to his left and make his shoulders and his whole body, look like he was going that way. The defensive back would commit and come in to try to make the tackle. Hornung was setting me up for the block and then he would go the other way. They were different runners, but both of them were sensational.

If they each rushed for 100 yards a game, then we were happy. It was always more of a team thing than an individual thing. We sure as hell were aware and happy about it.

Toughest Defensive Lineman
There are about five defensive linemen that I remember very well as being the toughest. Leo Nomellini, a great football player on the San Francisco 49ers, helped me out a great deal by putting his right foot back when he was going inside, and putting his feet parallel when he went outside. I picked that up my first year playing against him. From that point on, I knew everything that Leo was going to do and it made a huge difference in my blocking.

Art Donovan was a shaker and a matador. Most defensive tackles will come straight at you, bully you, try to run over you, or take you back to the quarterback. They'll use strength and aggression on you. Artie would stand up and shake. He would get his belly going side to side and he'd wait for you to make a lunge at him. Then he would step aside or grab you and push you in the direction that he'd want to go. Then he would go around you. I didn't understand that those kinds of tackles played in the NFL. The first time that I played against him, I wanted to hit him after the game to make sure that he was real. He was an education. All you had to do with him was wait on him. He couldn't shake forever. He had to make a move and when he made his move, you would move. You had to have patience.

Charlie Krueger played for the San Francisco 49ers, but he was from Texas. He was 6'5" and weighed 265. He was lean. He brought it all day and all night. He never slowed down for a play. He didn't take a half a play off. He didn't take a quarter of a play off. He just never let up.

The top two defensive linemen in my book were Merlin Olsen and Alex Karras. Merlin had great work ethic. He had great physical capabilities. He was 6'5".

I got Merlin and Doug Atkins on the scale one day at the Pro Bowl. They were giving me some crap about something and I said, "You two, get over here. I want to see what you weigh." They both got on the scale for me and one weighed 296 and one weighed 300. They were both listed at about 265, but that was a long way from reality.

Merlin never quit either. Merlin was going to be there until tomorrow night when you played against him. If you were going to try to whoop him, you better bring a light and a lunch, because it was going to take a while.

I was a finalist for the Pro Football Hall Of Fame in 1997. I still remember Art Daley calling me and doing a story about me. I said, "Well, Alex didn't play his heart out against Atlanta or the some of the other teams that weren't doing well that year. He played his heart out against Green Bay. He was fiery, angry, emotional, and he played his ass off. He was a hell of a football player." Art hung up from me and called Alex. He told Alex, "Kramer said you maybe didn't play all that hard against Atlanta and some of the lesser teams, and that you had a lot of animosity towards Green Bay. You had a lot of passion and a lot of fire; you were a different player." Alex said, "I'd say he's about right."

Alex was a wonderful football player. Alex had a low center of gravity. Merlin was 6'5". Tall boys got the strength up above. I don't think Alex was under 6'0", but it felt like he was 5'10" and 285. He just had a low center of gravity and he was really strong. He worked out all the time. He had a background in professional wrestling so he had the fire and the burn. He was a hell of a player.

Block On Jethro Pugh For Bart Starr On Game-Winning Quarterback Sneak In Ice Bowl
I had watched game film of the Dallas Cowboys' three previous games before our game. In their first game I saw Jethro Pugh was playing high in their goal line defense. The Cowboys defensive linemen put their noses about ten or twelve inches from the field. Bob Lilly would charge straight ahead and come low. You couldn't move him with a Caterpillar D9. Jethro was supposed to stay down low too.

The next game it's the same thing and the game after the same thing again. So I mentioned this to Coach Lombardi. I told Coach Lombardi, "We can wedge two if we have to." Coach Lombardi said in his most conversational, social voice, "What?"

I said, "I think we can wedge two if we have to." He said run that back to me. So I ran it back about four times to him. Coach Lombardi said, "That's right, put it in the red zone two."

I had no dream of that play being called on the one-yard line with 15 seconds to go. I thought Coach Lombardi might call it when we were on offense in the middle of the field or in the second quarter. I thought maybe we don't use it at all or we don't need it. I didn't think a lot about it.

We were a different team when we came down the field on that final drive against the Cowboys. Every guy was playing his ass off. So, now it was my turn. I knew what I needed to do and I prayed that Jethro was going to do what he did the last three weeks. So I find a little divot, almost like a golf divot, where my left foot would go. Normally I drove off my right foot. My right foot is back so I get more push off my right foot. My left shoe just snuggled into that divot so it acted like a starting block. I had a really good start when I came out of the crouch. In difficult situations, there are three things you really need to do. Keep your head up, your eyes open, and follow through. All I thought was, it's my responsibility since I suggested the play. It's on my back now, so let's get the job done. I kept my eyes open. Jethro came up and I put my face in his chest and everything worked out.

Green Bay Packers Rivalries

Coach Lombardi knew that the Green Bay Packers fans considered the Chicago Bears the ultimate rival. Coach Lombardi would say, "I'm going to go out there and beat those Bears. I want you to tear them up today. You guys beat the Bears and I tickle old man Halas' ass." Then Coach Lombardi would giggle a little bit.

We would have practice on Wednesday, Thursday, and Friday, and players would wear different jersey numbers when it was Bears week. I might wear number 12 and Bart might wear number 75.

Coach Lombardi would say, "Who's that guy down there? That's one of Halas' spies. Go see who it is. Go get his ID, show me who it is."

He was always using little gimmicks to get us interested in the game and pumped up about it. When I look back it was so silly. Could you imagine the Bears scout saying to Coach Halas, "They've got the fourth string playing quarterback. Number 75 is the quarterback this week." Not likely, you know. But it kind of got us going. It gave us a little lift, a little boost, and a little more animosity towards the Bears.

I think probably the Dallas Cowboys rivalry was more personal. Coach Lombardi and Coach Tom Laundry of the Cowboys didn't always agree on things when they were assistant coaches with the New York Giants. In the 1958 NFL Championship Game, Lombardi wanted to go for it on 4th down and Laundry wanted to punt. I believe there was always a personal thing there for Lombardi with Laundry.

Writing Book Instant Replay

Generally, I think the team's response was pretty positive when my book Instant Replay came out. The book had come out a week or two before training camp. We were in training camp and the book was getting a lot of conversation. I had a record that I liked to play before I went to sleep or as I was going to sleep called, One Stormy Night. The sound from the record was thunder, rain, and pitter-patter. It was mood music, kind of. I was playing the record and Gale Gillingham and Forrest Gregg were right across the hallway from me at Saint Norbert. I heard some stirring around in the hall. Gilly had gotten a glass, gone down to the john, and come into my room. He threw the water up on the ceiling so it was really raining. Gilly and Forrest were giggling their asses off. They thought it was really funny. Willie Davis was my roommate that year, and we didn't think it was quite as funny as they did. Willie said, "Be careful Forrest. Jerry will put that in his next book."

Forrest said, "That damn book. That's all I hear about. Everybody wants to know about that book. That damn book." He said, "I'll tell you one thing, Jerry. You were dead honest." I thought that was as high of praise as I could receive. He was not only my teammate; he was my linemate. He communicated with me like a brother. We were pretty close. When I saw something that was different I'd say, "Forrest, got it." When he'd see something he'd say, "Jerry." I'd say, "Yup."

That's all we'd say when an odd situation came up. So, I thought that was high praise from Forrest. I think generally the guys really enjoyed the book. It's been so much more than a book for me. I still get letters from people who are inspired by it. They took the Lombardi principles and it worked for them.

I met with the publisher, his people, and my agent in New York. I asked the publisher, "How many books do we need to sell to do good?" He said, "Jerry, 7,500 to 10,000. Sports books don't sell traditionally, so I think if we do 10,000 books, we will do well."

I never dreamt of ever writing a book or even being close to someone who wrote a book. I started to think that I had to use some big, long, flowery words that an author would use, and that I had better increase my vocabulary. I was having thoughts like that. That went on for two or three days. Then I thought, "Who do you think you're kidding? I mean, come on. It is what it is and you are who you are. So just be as dead honest as you can be about it.

Tell it exactly the way you see it and you think it is or could be. Be precise about what you say, because you're going to have to defend it. Be ready to defend it. If they don't like it, they don't like it, but at least you put it down the way you saw it to be and the way you thought it was." That was my final thought on that.

Playing Kicker & Offensive Line
Kicking puts a little pressure on you. It's a little bit of a different deal. You're all alone. The whole stadium is watching you. You can't think about all those things. You've just got to think about keeping your head down, following through, hitting the ball properly, and getting everything right. There was always a little nervousness with the kicking part of things. As an offensive lineman, my Momma didn't know what I was doing on the line.

People hardly ever saw you unless it was the Ice Bowl block or something like that. The big part was that you went unnoticed. That's what you really preferred as an offensive lineman—to go unnoticed. Kicking I felt was a responsibility and not a celebration. I wasn't tickled to death when I made a kick. I was relieved I had been able to do what the team wanted me to do. The last kick I made in Yankee Stadium in 1962, I knew exactly where we were and I knew that if I made that kick it would put the game pretty much out of reach.

The wind was blowing like hell. I aimed ten yards outside the right goal post and I kicked the ball. I hit it pretty solid and it came right down the middle of the goal post. I knew that they were asking me to do something and I had to get it done. I was more relaxed and pleased that I was able to make the kick than I was celebrating about the kick.

AFL-NFL World Championship Game "Super Bowl I"
We didn't give the Chiefs as much credit as they deserved in the AFL-NFL World Championship Game. We had no information about anybody they ever played. We had no way of judging them and their opponents. We watched films. We were watching a film one evening and two of their safeties ran into each other. Obviously one of them went the wrong way. They knocked each other down and were flat on their butts. One of the Green Bay Packers, Max McGee, starts doing Looney Tunes noises. We were giggling and laughing about it.

We thought the games would be in descending order of difficulty. That maybe the Rams would be the most difficult since they had beaten us three weeks before. The Cowboys would be right behind them since they had a good football team. Then we thought, we got the AFL-NFL World Championship Game and that will be the easiest game of the playoffs.

11

During the first quarter of the Championship Game we found out that there were some pretty damn good football players on the other side of the line for the Chiefs, including E.J. Holub, Ernie Ladd, Bobby Bell, Johnny Robinson, and Willie Lanier.

So we kind of checked our gear at halftime and buckled our hats. We came out of the locker room with a little bit of a different attitude, a much more serious attitude, and took care of business. We were not really that uptight or worried prior to the game. I think we were more worried at halftime than we were at the beginning of the game.

Green Bay Packers coach Vince Lombardi rides on the shoulders of tackle Forrest Gregg and guard Jerry Kramer (64) after defeating the Oakland Raiders in Super Bowl II. Photograph copyright Associated Press

Chapter 2

Bobby Beathard

College:
California Polytechnic State University

As Scout:
Kansas City Chiefs (1963, 1966-1967)
Atlanta Falcons (1968-1971)

As Executive:
Miami Dolphins (1972-1977)
Washington Redskins (1978-1988)
San Diego Chargers (1990-2000)

2018 Inductee Pro Football Hall Of Fame

Hiring By Kansas City Chiefs
The Kansas City Chiefs had an employee back then by the name of Don Klosterman. He knew how much I was involved with football and liked football. He knew that I played in high school and college. He wanted to know if I would be interested in scouting for him on the West Coast, in around 13 states. I said, "Sure, I'd love it."

Then, the Chiefs expanded my area. Later the Chiefs asked me to go to all around the country, just looking at the top prospects everywhere. It was something I was really excited about. It was kind of a natural thing for me.

Chiefs Owner Lamar Hunt was one of the nicest people I've ever known. It was a wonderful place to work.

Scouting In the (American Football League) AFL
Scouting in the AFL was kind of fun. We did things that they don't do now. The AFL and NFL were competing against each other. We were hiding players out where the NFL couldn't find them. The NFL was hiding players out where we couldn't find them. If you couldn't find a player and see him personally you wouldn't draft him. There were a lot of things going on like that, that don't go on anymore. It was a lot of fun. Looking back on it, it was a real exciting time in the league.

Kansas City Chiefs Winning AFL Championship
I don't know how to describe the Kansas City Chiefs winning the AFL Championship, but it was terrific. The three players from the team that come to mind right away are Curley Culp, Mike Garrett, and Jan Stenerud. It was great. The AFL was always the little brother league. It was something that wasn't at the level of the NFL. To be able to go up against the NFL and do well, that was a big step for that league.

14

Time With Atlanta Falcons
Tom Braatz was down in Atlanta with the Falcons and he brought me down there. We were friends. It was really a good thing for me to see how different organizations did things. I brought some things from the Chiefs that the Falcons wanted to know about. I learned things from the Falcons. It was fun. I was lucky. I tell my wife now that I got through life without a real job. I got to do something that I loved to do every day.

Working For Don Shula With Miami Dolphins
Working for Don Shula with the Miami Dolphins was great. I probably learned more working for Don than anybody. He said, "Okay, you're down here to get us players." He turned it over to me to do that and let me hire a scouting staff. I was never second-guessed or anything. He was the best. I'll tell you, the guy was just great. I really enjoyed my time there. I learned so much under Don that it really set me up for how to do things the rest of my career.

Don knew every aspect of the organization, to do with football. He could coach any position on the football team, offensively or defensively. He was a very demanding guy with the players. They all responded to the way he did it. He was just one of those guys that could get the best out of anybody.

When I look at some of the guys we had when we had the perfect season and when we won Super Bowls, I don't know if there's any other coach that could have done that with that group of players. I mean, they were good, but when I look at some of the later teams, I think maybe they weren't as good as these guys, man for man, but as a team, they were as good as anybody that had ever played.

On game days, Don told me, "You're not just going to sit in the stands and watch the game. You're going to do something." He had me working with special teams to make sure every special team player was ready to go in when we had to punt, or kickoff, or go for an extra point.

Don would say, "We have one player that no matter what, you always make sure you have his jersey in your hand when we call for special teams because he'll forget to go on the field."

One time, we sent the special teams on the field and I didn't even notice there were only 10 men on the field. Shula yelled and he knew exactly who wasn't on the field. He came over and grabbed me. I thought, "Oh my God!" I never made the mistake again.

Don Shula's Ability To Adapt
Don Shula and Joe Gibbs could adapt to anything. When a key player would go down, some coaches would say, "Oh, no. Now what do we do?" Shula wouldn't bat an eye. He'd say, "Hey, we're going to be fine." Jim Del Gaizo came in at quarterback and won games for the Miami Dolphins. Nothing bothered Don Shula. He'd say, "We're going to go on. We're fine. All our backups are as good as our starters." It was just amazing how he handled it. I've been with teams where somebody got hurt and coaches would show it bothered them. It affects the players, but it never affected Shula. Shula never let it show or affect the players.

Miami Dolphins Offensive Line
The Miami Dolphins had a great offensive line. Those guys would have been great today. Monte Clark was a great offensive line coach. When you look at Jim Langer, Bob Kuechenberg, and all those guys, they were terrific.

Losing Paul Warfield, Larry Csonka, & Jim Kiick To World Football League (WFL)

It was tough when Paul Warfield, Larry Csonka, and Jim Kiick left the Miami Dolphins for the World Football League (WFL). Thinking of the money the WFL was throwing around, I just didn't think the WFL would make it. Of course, it didn't. It was tough to lose those guys.

Don Shula was amazing in that anything that happened that was bad, he didn't want to address it or talk about it. It was like nothing happened. His viewpoint was "We're just going to go on. We're going to be better now than we ever were". He could get his point across, where everybody felt, "You know, it's not a big deal. We're going to be fine. We have other guys that can do as well." Son of a gun, we would! He was just an amazing guy, that anything bad that happened, you never dwelled on it. It was, look at the good side of things and we'll be better.

1972 Miami Dolphins Perfect Season

It got harder for the Miami Dolphins team as they approached the end of the 1972 season. Every team that the Dolphins played had more incentive to win that game than anything because we hadn't lost a game. There was also a lot more pressure on our team. It was just amazing how that team could go through and do it. I don't think it will ever be done again. I watch the NFL closely every year, looking at all the teams, and I just don't think it's likely.

Earl Morrall Replacing An Injured Bob Griese During 1972 Perfect Season

The most amazing thing during the 1972 Miami Dolphins season was when Bob Griese went down, we won with Earl Morrall. I really think Earl was a great person. I liked Earl and he was a good quarterback. Earl wasn't what Griese was, nor a Marino type or anything like that. Earl wasn't the quarterback that you thought would take you to the Super Bowl.

Don Shula did things a little different with Earl than he would with Griese. Sure enough, we pulled it off. It was just amazing. I think the things that Don did in cases like that were just amazing. I don't know if many coaches could do that.

Decision To Work For Washington Redskins

I decided to leave the Miami Dolphins for the Washington Redskins because I was given more responsibility. It was just a step up, I thought. I talked to Don Shula, about it. Don said, "You know, that's a great opportunity." It was. Maybe he was trying to get rid of me, I don't know. It was one of those things. He encouraged me to go. I didn't want to go. I said, "I don't want to leave here. I've grown up by the beach all my life." He said, "No. You ought to go for the interview. Go and meet them and see what it's like."

I went to Washington and met with Edward Bennett Williams, the Redskins Owner. Edward was such a nice guy. After the interview, he offered me the job. I went back to Don and said, "You know what? I'm going to take the job. It's going to be different, but it will be fun."

Rebuilding the Washington Redskins

With the Redskins I went into a situation where their prior philosophy was completely different from mine. I wanted to build through the draft. During the recently completed George Allen Era, George was keeping all the old veterans and would always trade for old veterans and forget about the draft. Washington didn't have any draft choices when I went there. George traded them all away for veterans. I had a whole different philosophy to build thru the draft. I've got old letters and hate mail for getting rid of some of the old veterans that had won for George.

The old guys weren't required to do the work that you have to do in football. George had his way of winning. I just had a different philosophy. There was a lot of pressure on me in Washington because of getting rid of all the old guys. The Redskin fans hated me for getting rid of those guys. The players wanted lifetime jobs and to get all that money. Even though they weren't at the level to play in the NFL anymore and win.

When I go back to Redskins reunions every year, I still see a lot of those guys. I always go out with Sonny Jurgensen, Billy Kilmer, and a lot of those guys, and have a lot of fun talking about those days.

I pretty much had a plan in my head, what I had to do. You have to look at what the prospects are in the draft. Is it a strong year for offensive lines? If it just happened to be that, we drafted a lineman.

Plus, you have to have the right coaches. I've been with teams where if you draft a guy in the tenth round, the coach has already got in his mind, "No tenth rounder is going to make our team." We had a coach where it didn't matter if we drafted someone in the tenth or eleventh round, or if a player wasn't even drafted and we signed him as a free agent. My agreement with the coaches was to give all players the same opportunity they would give a first round pick. We had a lot of kids that weren't drafted, or were drafted late, make it and do well.

The best example I can think of is when we took Darrell Green as last pick in the first round. I had scouted him prior to the draft. I called Darrell to tell him we had drafted him. He said, "Bobby why did you take so long to take me?" I said, "Well, that's where we had a pick because we won the Super Bowl. We didn't have a pick that early in the round.

Don't blame me. Look at all the other teams that passed you up."

Darrell came in and Richie Petitbon, our secondary coach said, "Bobby, a guy that small can't play in this league." I said, "Well, this guy's different." Darryl played around 18 years in the NFL.

Joe Gibbs

I had a good friend, Ernie Zampese. Ernie and I used to talk a lot. Ernie had coached with Joe Gibbs for a long time. Joe was coaching with Don Coryell. I liked Coryell's style of football. Ernie and I had talked about Joe before. I called Ernie and said, "What do you think? Is Joe ready to be a head coach?" Ernie said, "Joe's ready now." I called Joe and said, "Hey, will you take the job if I get to pick you?" He said, "Yes." I said, "Okay, figure out who you want on your offensive staff and keep our defense staff." He said, "Okay."

Jack Kent Cooke called me in his office and said, "Okay. What are we going to do about head coach?" I said, "Well, I've already got a guy." He said, "What do you mean you got a guy?" I said, "I got a guy to be our coach." He said, "Who you thinking of?" I said, "Well, you don't know him. You haven't heard of him. This guy named Joe Gibbs." He said, "Joe Gibbs! Who in the hell is Joe Gibbs?" He said, "They'll crucify me if I bring a guy in here named Joe Gibbs. Nobody knows who he is." I said, "I know they don't. That's the good thing about him. Everybody isn't after him. It will be fine."

Mr. Cooke let me hire him. Joe put the offensive staff together and kept the defensive staff. Then, we went on to lose our first three games. I would go out of town, usually on Tuesday mornings to go to different colleges around the country scouting. I would look at the game film on Monday with the coaches, and go out Tuesday scouting and come back Friday night. Mr. Cooke called me and said, "I want you to get out to my house right away." I said, "I can't. I've got to go scouting." He said, "Do you own this team?" I said, "No, sir." He said, "You cancel your plans and get out to my house now." I had to drive all the way out to where he lived. He sat me down and said, "I should fire you and that coach you hired."

After we lost a couple games Mr. Cooke said, "You bring your coach out here with you." I go into the offensive room and say, "Joe you got to go to Mr. Cooke's." He said, "I can't. We're doing game plan." I told him Mr. Cooke was not giving him a choice. Mr. Cooke chewed Joe and I both out and sent us back home. It was awful for the first five games.

Then, we started winning. Later on Mr. Cooke would tell Joe, "You're the coach I always wanted. The first thing I told Bobby was, "You get Joe Gibbs. That's the guy we want." Joe and I still, to this day, laugh about that.

John Riggins
John Riggins had quit football. The funny thing is that when I used to go to colleges scouting, I had met John's sister. She was a secretary at the coach's office at the University of Kansas. I called her and said, "Hey, this is Bobby calling. I want to know if you can set it up so I can come out there and meet with John." I had met John before. I had a decent relationship with him, and he trusted me.

I flew out there and saw his sister. Then she set up the meeting so I could talk to John. I met privately with John and said, "Hey, look it, it's all different. It's not the George Allen thing anymore. This is Joe Gibbs; just give it a try. The best thing I can do is have Joe come over here and to meet you personally, and you'll trust him." I had Joe come over and meet with John. John agreed that he would play for Joe. That was the way we got John to come back to the Redskins.

Decision To Leave Washington Redskins
My mom and dad were getting old and living in California and I missed them. They used to go to Washington for a game each year, but they were getting to an age where they didn't want to travel. I wanted to be near them. We were really close. They were getting way up there in age. That was the reason that I left. That was the only reason.

Mr. Cooke told me to not go to another team for a year. I agreed to sit out a year. Then I got a call from NFL Network to broadcast for them. I was at NFL Network for a year and then joined the San Diego Chargers.

Decision To Retire
The travel, going everywhere in the country looking for players, was starting to get to me. I was never home much. I thought, "Is this what I want to do the rest of my life?" I didn't want to draft players I hadn't seen personally. If I couldn't travel and see them, and could only see them on tape, I thought it was time for me to do something else and retire. I had kids and I wanted to see them play their Friday night games and all that stuff. A lot of things went into the decision. It was a pretty easy decision.

Most general managers stayed in the office. I was one of the few general managers that went all around the country all football season, looking for players. I don't know many general managers who wanted to do that. I was afraid not to do it because I wanted to see the players in practice and do all the other stuff before we ever drafted them. That's why I made the deal that I'd be the general manager, but I still wanted to go out all season and look at players. I'd come back every weekend for the games.

Dexter Manley

Dexter Manley was a heck of a player. Dexter was a fun guy to be around. He practiced like it was an actual game. It was tough for any offensive tackle to handle him in practice. He was just a screwball. He practiced hard every day. He gave the offensive linemen a real picture of what a game was like. That guy was, he was really something. I would have hated to be an offensive tackle to have to play against Dexter every week.

Photograph copyright Associated Press

Chapter 3

Jimmy Johnson

College: UCLA
Career History: San Francisco 49ers (1961-1976)
1994 Inductee Pro Football Hall of Fame

College Choice

The main reason I chose UCLA was the fact that my brother Rafer had chosen UCLA for his college sports career. Rafer was a senior in high school when I was a freshman. I watched his career as it progressed, and was very excited that I had the opportunity to go to UCLA.

My decision to go to Santa Monica City School for my first year of college boiled down to, from my point of view as an athlete, it giving me an opportunity to work against a tougher level of football player. As a freshman at UCLA, I would have only been playing against freshman from other schools. Also, the freshmen at UCLA only played five games during the season. In addition, Santa Monica City School gave me an opportunity to up my game in a couple of academic classes.

College Coaches

Red Sanders was Head Coach at UCLA, and I was expecting to play under his tutelage. Unfortunately, he passed away.

George Dickerson took over when Coach Sanders passed away. That created a monumental pressure, recruiting and what not, on Coach Dickerson.

He had a nervous breakdown from the recruiting wars, trying to talk high school players into coming to UCLA. Billy Barnes took over and was at UCLA for my last two years of college.

Playing On Offense & Defense In College

I actually preferred to play on offense. In the single wing formation that we used at UCLA, I was in the wing back slot. The wing back slot didn't really get to carry the ball that much. From that position I would be flanked out and become a part of the passing game. I would run a reverse a couple of times a game.

In the wing back position on any given play, I was usually scraping along the line and blindsiding offensive linemen.

Playing Against USC

USC was definitely our biggest rival. It was a monumental situation for someone like me. I went to UCLA via Kingsburg High School in the Central Valley. Kingsbury was a very small high school and we played in front of very small high school crowds. Playing against USC was a very overpowering experience. What I think worked in my behalf was the fact that I went to Santa Monica City College my freshman year.

I had a very nice season at Santa Monica City College, both academically and in sports. It gave me a chance to play three sports for one more year. I played football, basketball, and ran track and field. That was the first time I ran track and field.

Running Track & Field At UCLA
When I left Santa Monica City College I no longer played competitive basketball. I actually was not going to run track; but was just going to play football at UCLA. UCLA had a renowned coach by the name of Ducky Drake. Ducky convinced me that if I stuck with track and field, I could be a world- class runner by the time I got out of UCLA.

I took him at his word and participated in track with the football department's good wishes. I didn't have to attend spring football training I just ran track. Ducky's words rang true as I had a pretty fantastic track and field career.

Not Qualifying For 1960 US Olympic Team
It was absolutely devastating not qualifying for the 1960 Olympic team. That was probably the most devastating situation for me because my brother was going to be on the team competing. I had progressed during my last two track seasons in college to a world premier level. I was running good times at UCLA under the tutelage of Coach Ducky Drake. I was really primed to make that Olympic team.

After the NCAA finals, which were held at UC Berkley, I ran in some AAU meets and ran some really phenomenal times. The Olympic trials came down to that last big meet which was held at Stanford University. I won a couple of prelims at the trials. I got to the finals as the number one seed. I had a middle lane, right smack in the middle of the track.

I led the race for seven hurdles. I hit the seventh hurdle and nicked the eighth hurdle but regained my balance. I was in a photo finish. Now when you're in a photo finish, you find out the results right away.

Back then, they had to develop the film and make a decision. It wasn't a real quick process. There was a lot of waiting around until I got the final results of the race. It was a photo finish between Hayes Jones, Jerry Tarr, Lee Calhoun, and me. I didn't qualify for the Olympics.

There went my aspirations to become an Olympian. In my mind, I went back to what Ducky Drake had told me when I was a sophomore at UCLA. He told me that if I worked at it, I could become a world- class hurdler. I was one step short of making the 1960 Olympic Games.

Draft
There was talk that I was going to be drafted. I just continued on with my college life at UCLA, not really thinking that I would be drafted.

A lot of things happened for the dominoes to fall into place. The 49ers had sent out feelers to try to find out if I would be interested in playing for them. That was a no brainer. Of course I was interested. Later on I found out the L. A. Rams and the San Diego Chargers were also interested.

Sid Gillman
Coach Gilman was a real cheerleader in reference to my situation. I had several meetings with Al Davis and Coach Gilman in Los Angeles.

There were a lot of ifs and buts in what the Chargers and the 49ers were going to do. The morning of the draft, I was having breakfast with Sid Gilman and Al Davis in their hotel suite at the Stanford campus. It was all lined up, if such and such is still available, then this will happen and this will happen.

As it turned out the 49ers had three first round draft picks that year. They had the Pittsburgh Steelers number one pick, the St. Louis Cardinals number one pick, and their own. They ended up using a first round pick on me. With their other two first round picks they got Billy Kilmer and Bernie Casey.

Al Davis and Sid Gillman were very excited about the possibility of me playing for them and I was equally excited. There was a little overlay of aw shucks, when the 49ers drafted me. I finished my breakfast with them and went back over to the campus to continue my preparation for the East-West game.

Red Hickey
It was hard to understand where Coach Hickey was coming from. With his military background, he treated the team from top to bottom like we were recruits in the Army. He had a very tough approach and would let you know exactly how he felt. That was one good thing about him.

If you were on his down side, he would verbally let you know. In the middle of a practice he'd stop the practice and he'd use all of these red-hot words. He would just jump all over the perpetrator on the team that had made a mistake. It was almost like he was steaming.

College All-Star Game
I played in the East-West Shrine Game, Coaches All-America Game in Buffalo, New York, and then I went to Chicago to start preparing for the College All-Star Game. The Philadelphia Eagles were the previous season's NFL Champion, so that was who we were going to face off against in the game.

We practiced at the Northwestern College Campus in Evanston, Illinois. I was strictly an offensive end on the team. I had real good speed and good hands. I was beating a lot of guys out there in one-on-one situations.

There was a defensive back, Elbert Kimbrough, who had also been drafted by the 49ers, like me. I was having a really super day during one practice. Elbert had to cover me on several occasions. Billy Kilmer was the quarterback. On a post pattern, I beat Elbert really bad and I was just waiting for the ball to come to me since Billy had thrown a floater. While waiting for the floater, Elbert made up the yardage that I had beat him by and really took me out with a tremendous tackle. I dislocated my wrist and broke my arm. They put my arm in a cast and I was not able to be a participant in the game.

Rookie Season With 49ers
I went to the 49ers training camp with a broken arm. It was apparent that I wasn't going to be able to play on offense my rookie year. The 49ers team physician, Dr. Lloyd Milburn, told me if I wanted to play my rookie year that he would take my dislocated left wrist and re-work the bones by using pressure.

He operated on me on two different occasions, attempting to put the wrist bones back in position. It was readily known I wouldn't be able to play on offense. I recovered well enough that with proper protection on the wrist, I was able to play a defensive back for the 49ers.

've surprised myself with my ability in man-to-man coverage. A lot of times I had inside help from our outside linebackers, and some deep help from the free safety. For the most part, I was on my own in figuring out the opponent's wide receivers.

Many times I was in a flanked out position with the receiver, 20 yards from the line of scrimmage with very little help. Even with a broken arm, I learned a lot about myself as a man- to-man cover guy during my rookie year. Those first few years I was an excellent man-to-man guy and that worked in my behalf as my career got rolling along.

After a few seasons, I could hold my own against a premier wide receiver like Charley Taylor of the Washington Redskins, knowing that I wasn't going to get a lot of help from my teammates. During my career, quarterbacks would not throw my way. During a game I may have gotten two balls thrown my way. Quarterbacks would work the other side.

Gale Sayers Knee Injury Against 49ers
Kermit Washington, being a real tough tackler, caught Gale Sayers when Gale was making a cut. Gale was making a real sharp cut, changing direction and unfortunately Kermit's shoulder pad and helmet hit Gale right on the knee and hyperextended the knee with such force that Gale's knee broke down.

Toughest Receiver
 never categorized a wide receiver as the best. I knew that every Sunday my game plan was going to be full just trying to take care of the wide receiver I was matched up against.

There were a lot of wonderful wide receivers. If there was one guy that I had an affinity to work against and be competitive, it was Tommy McDonald. Tommy played on the Philadelphia Eagles and later on in his career with the L.A. Rams. In a highly competitive football game Tommy would do a few comical things on the football field and I couldn't figure out why he was doing those things. The main thing was just to stay close to him. He had great speed and jackrabbit like moves.

We were playing the Rams and Tommy ran a pattern on me, and I blocked it. Tommy ran another one and I blocked it. When you block a pass pattern, you tend to want to lounge a little bit, get up slow, and feel good about the fact that you just knocked a ball down. On that first pass pattern that I blocked, Tommy jumped up from the ground and ran just as fast back to the huddle as he was running on the pass pattern.

 thought he was doing that to psych me out. In order to be in position, I jumped up just as fast as he did, and ran back towards the line of scrimmage with the same vigor and speed that he had run the pattern. I found out later in that game that was just the way Tommy was, like a little jackrabbit.

Jack Christiansen Being Named 49ers Head Coach
Jack Christiansen had been my defensive backfield coach with the 49ers, so I was a little bit sad to lose him as my defensive back coach when he became our head coach. He worked very closely with me in deference to my ability as a defensive back. Red Hickey got fired as head coach. Coach Hickey was such a tyrant. He had us all walking on our heels. If a player was walking down the hallway in the dorm and saw Hickey down the

hallway, he would rather go the other way so he wouldn't have to run into Coach Hickey.

When you would see him in the hallway, it was a very high tension, stringent situation. Almost everyone tried to avoid eye contact or speaking with Coach Hickey as they moved about the dorms. He made it really difficult.

The players loved Coach Christensen. Everybody wanted to win for him. We had been under the iron fist of Coach Hickey for so long that I think the players, as much as they wanted to win for the coach, just couldn't quite put their nose to the grindstone because of Coach Hickey.

When Coach Christiansen was named head coach, players started doing silly things like not being on time, missing a meeting, and not getting treatment. We just couldn't get a victory. The harder we tried the less likely it was that we'd get a victory. I think the reason for us not winning under Coach Christiansen was that is was like a bunch of guys getting out of jail or out of the Army; all of a sudden you are able to just spread your wings and fly on your own. There were a lot of infractions the players committed. Things that they could have done easily, they just didn't do. The team just didn't play the type of ball that Coach Christenson deserved as head coach.

Dick Nolan
Dick Nolan brought in a whole different regimen. It was very much together. Everyone knew what he had to do to be a part of a winning effort, from the front office right on down to the water boy.

Everyone got onboard. We were primed to do a two hundred percent job all day every day. Coach Nolan was an easy head coach to be around. He was a great guy.

Coach Nolan had the complete package with his coaching staff and with each individual. He had a personal relationship, or as close as you could get. Players felt Coach Nolan was their buddy.

You would never walk up and throw your arms around his neck or give him a bear hug, but that's the way you felt about him. You knew what he was trying to do; the avenue he was taking it. We all knew that we were potential champions.

Pro Football Hall Of Fame Induction
When I found out I was being inducted into the Pro Football Hall Of Fame it was pretty monumental. I experienced a lot of disbelief. I didn't think it was going to happen. I didn't think that I could garner the votes necessary. My family and I were very excited. I think what made it even more exciting was the fact that local media came by my house to talk about it.

It was almost like I had an extension of my career. There was a lot written about me being chosen. A lot of people said a lot of nice things on my behalf. I was beside myself. I was extremely happy it finally happened.

My family and brothers and sisters were extremely ecstatic. The letters I got congratulating me really brought it to the forefront. It was a long road, but I was very happy that it finally became a reality.

San Francisco 49er Jimmy Johnson plays bump and run coverage on Los Angeles Rams wide receiver Jack Snow. Photograph copyright Associated Press

Chapter 4

Mel Blount

College:
Southen

Career History:
Pittsburgh Steelers (1970-1983)

1989 Inductee Pro Football Hall Of Fame

College Choice

I grew up during segregation and when I came out of high school in 1966, the University of Georgia, Georgia Tech, Alabama and all of those types of schools weren't recruiting black athletes. I had an opportunity to go to schools like Savannah State, Albany State, Fort Valley State, and Southern University. Southern University just happened to hear about me and came recruiting me. That's why I decided to go there.

Southern University is in Baton Rouge, Louisiana. I was in Georgia, but there was an official who officiated one of my games my senior year in high school. He knew some people at Southern University. Well, the night that he officiated my high school game, I scored five touchdowns.

I was a kickoff returner, wide receiver, and defensive end. I was able to get into the end zone five times, so I obviously made an impression on the official. The official knew some people at Southern University and told them about me. They came and offered me a scholarship.

Head Coach Eddie Robinson Of Grambling

Believe it or not, Southern University was more popular than Grambling. Southern was a bigger, historically black, college than Grambling. Eddie Robinson did get some great players and so did Southern. Southern didn't have the stability at the coaching position that Grambling had because even when I was there we had a turnover at a head coach. Eddie Robinson was at Grambling for a long period of time and was able to build a tremendous program.

NFL Draft

I had never really heard of anybody on the Steelers. I did see the Steelers play the New Orleans Saints when I was still in college in 1969. When the Steelers drafted me, I had no idea who they had on their team. I had never heard of Joe Greene, who had been drafted in 1969. I didn't know the Steelers were going to draft me. I was somewhat disappointed when they did.

I wanted to play for the New Orleans Saints obviously because I was in Louisiana. I just thought that would have been a great team to play for, but little did I know that God had different plans for me. I was a

28

third round pick and I felt like most players do after being drafted, that I should have gone higher in the draft. But it all worked out.

Chuck Noll

Chuck Noll came to the Pittsburgh Steelers with a plan that he was going to build his team through the draft and it was going to take some time. My rookie year, Terry Bradshaw was the Steelers first round pick in the NFL draft. Ron Shanklin, a wide receiver from North Texas State, the same school Joe Greene went to, was the Steelers second round pick. I was the Steelers third round pick. We all came in and we made contributions to the organization. In fact, I think all of us at some point were All-Pros.

Chuck started acquiring players, through the draft, to build a championship team. Certainly there were expectations. The Steelers were at the bottom of the barrel in the NFL. They really were the doormat of the National Football League, so there was only one direction that they could go, and that was up.

Chuck was a fair coach. He was tough and demanding, but I thought he was fair and very detail oriented. He was just a great coach. I think he was the reason that so many of us were not only All- Pros, but wound up in the Pro Football Hall Of Fame. He made you want to be the best you could be.

Chuck wanted his players to be professionals on the field, family men off the field, and good community leaders. He was a tremendous leader and had a tremendous amount of influence on my life. I think any player you talk to that played for Chuck would tell you the same thing. He didn't get the kind of notoriety that Vince Lombardi got, but he was right there in that same class.

Pittsburgh Steelers Players Mentality

There's a thing called accountability. I think every player wanted to be held accountable and wanted to make sure that they didn't disappoint their teammates. It was a tremendous thing to be a part of. So much respect and love grew out of that because when you're out on the football field, you have to believe in the guy that you're lined up next to. I think that was the thing that really separated us in the '70s from the rest of the teams. Every guy wanted to make sure that he didn't disappoint the next guy.

Leader Of Pittsburgh Steelers Defense

The Pittsburgh Steelers whole defense was built around Joe Greene. When you talk about leaders, a leader to me is whoever will go out there and make a play for you. I think in the sense of being recognized by the public, the fans, or the front office, Joe Greene was the leader without a doubt. That was his team. That was his defense.

Joe Greene

To me, Joe Greene looked like he played angry all the time. Joe wants to make people believe that he didn't deserve the name Mean Joe Greene, but Joe Greene was something man. He was just a tremendous player. He was also a guy that didn't mind getting into fights or getting in your grill. I'm not just talking about the guys that he played with. I'm talking about the opponents, too. On the banquet circuit, everybody's got a Joe Greene story.

Playing Cornerback In NFL

Chuck Noll put me where he thought I could help the team the most, and that was playing 14 years at the cornerback position. I led the league in 1975 with 11 interceptions. I became the Pittsburgh Steelers all time interception leader, so I can't complain about the position I played. I just wanted to be a great player whether it was at safety, cornerback, or wherever they put me on special teams. I just wanted to be out there making a contribution.

Being successful starts with attitude. It starts with just wanting to be the best. You must have a willingness to work and do the things that will help you get better. I've always said, there's no substitute for hard work. I don't care how talented you are. I enjoyed the game. I enjoyed the preparation. I enjoyed working during the off-season and getting ready for training camp … the whole process.

"Mel Blount Rule" Established By NFL In 1977 A Receiver Can Only Be Bumped By Defender Within Five Yards Of the Line Of Scrimmage

When the NFL passed the rule change, it just made me raise my game to prove that I could do more than bump and run. We went on to win two more Super Bowls after that. After the rule change, I still played the bump and run within five yards. It's a compliment any time a player can have an impact on the game that they start legislating the game to slow you down, or to takeaway what they would call your aggressiveness.

I also think the Steelers were so dominant, the NFL decided to take away the head slap and all those other things that Joe Greene, L.C. Greenwood, and those guys were doing on the defensive line. We were just talented people.

Paul Brown was on the competition committee and he was going against us twice a year as Owner of the Cincinnati Bengals. He had seen enough. So he wanted to see what he could do to change the rules and help free up Isaac Curtis. But after all that, we still performed at a high level.

Toughest Wide Receiver

All the wide receivers I faced were tough. When you get into the National Football League, there is no cakewalk. I think one of the things that helped us, and I'm talking about myself and the guys who played in the secondary with me, was that we played against the best every day in practice. So we when got up against a Charlie Joiner or Paul Warfield, you know those kind of guys, we knew how to play and we knew what we needed to do. Well they all were tough. We were prepared because we were going against the best every day in practice in John Stallworth and Lynn Swann.

Pittsburgh Steelers Practices

I think what separated us from a lot of teams is that our starting defense practiced against our starting offense. I think that's why we were dominant and won four Super Bowl championships. Nobody was above anybody on our team. I don't care if you were a special teams player or if you were Mel Blount or Joe Greene. We all went out there to work and to get better. The only way you can get better is to go out against the best. So, the first team defense always went against the first team offense. That might have been one of the secrets to the Steelers, and the way they operated.

Super Bowl IX Pittsburgh Steelers vs. Minnesota Vikings First Steelers Super Bowl

For me our first Super Bowl was a tremendous experience. It was also a confirmation of what kind of team we had. A lot of people said we shouldn't have been there and that we weren't going to win because we were playing the "Purple People Eaters." They said we got lucky against the Oakland Raiders. I think ur winning that Super Bowl was not only a confirmation, but it was an eye opener to the rest of the league about who the Pittsburgh Steelers were and where we were going.

Favorite Super Bowl

My favorite team to play against in the Super Bowl was the Cowboys. There was so much motivation because they were being promoted as America's team. It was what they call bulletin board material against the opponents. So, I think they were my favorite.

I think our toughest Super Bowl was against the Los Angeles Rams. The Rams were the team we went in trailing to at halftime. Our offense with John Stallworth, Lynn Swann, and Terry Bradshaw kind of opened things up in the second half and we were able to get out of there with a victory. They played a good game against us.

Intercepting Roger Staubach In Super Bowl XIII

My interception of Roger Staubach in Super Bowl XIII was a big play. It was a big play right before halftime since the Cowboys were driving. Any time you can stop a drive it's a big play. Every time I see Roger, he relives that play. He asks me what I saw on that play.

When you have that many great athletes on the field, a lot of things happen. I was fortunate enough to be able to read the play and jump in and get the interception. That really stopped their momentum. It allowed us to go into halftime with the lead.

Decision To Retire

I decided to retire because I had just gotten tired mentally and I wasn't enjoying the game anymore. It's interesting because I had another year on my contract that would have paid me more money than I had made all of my years, but I just wasn't there. I have never been the kind of guy that hung around just to hang on. I had my own standards. I didn't need anybody to tell me just to come back and be a part. My standards are my standards and I don't lower them for anybody. It was time and I knew it from a mental standpoint. Physically, my body was fine. I was just tired mentally.

Pro Football Hall Of Fame Induction

Being inducted into the Pro Football Hall Of Fame was really something that I never thought about. When it happened, it took awhile for it to sink in about what it really meant. I'm grateful for the guys I played with, because you don't get there by yourself. We are all standing on somebody's shoulders. It was a tremendous thing. I don't know if anybody can ever explain the feeling to you.

When I came to the Pittsburgh Steelers, even when I retired, I never thought about the Hall Of Fame, let alone being selected in my first year of eligibility. It's just something that you didn't think about in those days because they didn't talk about it on television like they do now. Now everybody is a future Hall Of Famer, if you listen to the commentators. I'm sure guys who retire now think about it. When I played, it wasn't even mentioned.

Being Called Greatest Cornerback Of All-Time

I don't know if I'm the greatest; I haven't heard that too much. I think Gil Brandt just did a list and listed me as being the sixth best cornerback in the history of the game. So everybody has his or her own opinion. The only thing I know is that I played the best I could play. I was part of four world championships and made the Pro Bowl numerous times.

I don't have a real problem when somebody says, "Hey, so-and-so was better than you," or "They list you as number six or number four or whatever …" I think what's important is that you played the best you could play. You left the game and went on to do something to help people become better. Helping people who are less fortunate, that's what it's all about. Just trying to make the world a better place than what you found it.

Pittsburgh Steelers Mel Blount hauls in Houston Oiler running back Earl Campbell for no gain.
Photograph copyright Associated Press

Chapter 5

Robert Brazile

College:
Jackson State

Career History:
Houston Oilers (1975-1984)

2018 Inductee Pro Football Hall Of Fame

College Choice
When I came out of high school, which was back in the '70s, I originally signed with Troy State. Troy State is one of the major colleges in Alabama. Rickey Young was a very good friend of mine. We had grown up together and we wanted to go to the same college. So, we took a bus trip up to Troy State for a visit and we each signed a letter of intent with Troy State. We thought we were going to end up playing there, but my mom and my dad wanted to see the college that I had chosen.

We went up to Troy State at the wrong time of the year, which was spring. All the people were out sun tanning. My momma drove up to the campus and said, "Well, that will tell you one thing." She looked at Rickey, my dad, and me, and said, "Turn the car around. They need to find another school, there's nobody going to school here." So, that ended me going to Troy State. I think there were too many naked people laying around on the campus for my momma.

I had a cousin who played at Jackson State. He had told Jackson State Head Football Coach Bob Hill, that he had a couple of guys that wanted to come visit. So, we went over to visit Bob the following Saturday.

Bob wasn't interested in Robert Brazile; he was interested in Rickey Young. He looked down at Rickey's legs and said, "You play football?" Rickey said, "Yeah." They had a good conversation and Bob signed Rickey. I asked him, "What about me, coach?" He said, "Well, you come on. You've got pretty good confidence." So that's how I ended up at Jackson State.

Jackson State
Playing at Jackson State was a challenge when you look at what we did and what we had to go through during the '70s in the SWAC Conference. The SWAC had a bunch of great athletes from Grambling, Texas Southern, Prairie View, Alcorn, and Mississippi Valley. After my senior year, we had eight guys go to the pros. Before that, Jackson State had four or five guys go pro and even before that, they had two or three. We had talent on the field every day.

Walter Payton
Walter Payton and I roomed a little bit on the road as well as on campus. We had three to a room.

I played against some great athletes coming out of Mobile, and I played against some great running backs during my college career. Walter was an exceptional, different type of athlete. Walter could do anything he wanted to with a football, a basketball, or anything that involved a ball. Walter could do it. I saw Walter grow up and mature.

People ask me all the time, "What made you such a great pursuer and also a great tackler?" I say, "If I could just get my hands on Walter, I could make a great tackle." Just to get my hands on him. I'm not talking about getting him down, just being able to touch him. When you touch a gifted guy like Walter everyday, it betters your game and your program.

NFL Draft
I thought that the Dallas Cowboys were going to draft me. All I wanted to do was just hit players and prove my ability. I just wanted to be drafted by a team. Rickey Young always want to go to the West Coast. Walter Payton just wanted to play. I think he wanted to be a Chicago Bear. I just wanted to go play professional football.

College All-Star Game
Playing in the College All-Star Game was quite an experience. We trained with the Super Bowl Champion Pittsburgh Steelers. We lined up against these champs and were told we had a good team of players. The College All-Stars all thought, "Hey this our chance to shine." We led the Steelers during the game and Joe Gilliam of the Steelers asked, "What are you guys trying to do?"

The Steelers made a couple of touchdowns in the second half and beat us. I really thought we were going beat the Steelers. It was a great experience for me. I was ready for the Houston Oilers training camp when I got there. I knew what to expect.

Bum Phillips
Bum Phillips is one of the coaches I think should be in the Pro Football Hall Of Fame. Bum was one of the best coaches I play under. I played for some coaches that I admired and respected. My high school coaches were great coaches.

My college coach, Bob Hill, was a drill sergeant. He would work us to death. As a matter of fact, when I got to the pros, I was thinking, "Is this all we're going do?" After a couple of days, I got a chance to build and go on.

You earned Bum's respect when you respected him. It was a total father-like situation. You could go to Bum and ask him anything, and he would give you a truthful answer. It was probably the answer you wanted to hear.

One day I said to him, "Bum, I need to go home. We are having Fathers' Day in Mobile, Alabama." Bum asked, "Can you be back the next day?" I said, "Yes." Bum said, "Then go to your folks." He was one of the most lovable and understanding coaches, a professional would want to play under.

Houston Oilers 3-4 Defense
Bum Phillips knew what he wanted when he put that 3-4 defense together. On one side of me was a Pro Football Hall Of Famer in Elvin Bethea, and next to him was another Pro Football Hall Of Famer in Curley Culp. On the other side there was Tody Smith. A lot of people forget about my strong side linebacker, Teddy Washington. Teddy Washington was one of the strongest strong side linebackers

that I'd ever seen play the game, and that's taking nothing away from anyone else in the NFL. Teddy Washington was great.

We had Teddy holding up everything on his side and Elvin and me on the right side most of the time, coming up on the offense. It's hard to perceive that but it's what we had. Bum drafted the people that he needed for his 3-4 defense. It started with Curley Culp who was the best nose guard. We had Elvin and me on the same side. Gregg Bingham, Steve Kiner, and Teddy Washington played linebacker. That was one great 3-4 defense.

Rivalry Between Houston Oilers & Dallas Cowboys

The rivalry between the Houston Oilers & Dallas Cowboys started before I got to Houston. Bum came to the Oilers and put together a great group of guys. He traded John Matuszak for Curley Culp. He got other players, like me, thru the draft.

We were still under the shadow of a winning organization in the Cowboys. The Cowboys had six future Pro Football Hall Of Famers playing for them all out of the Houston area. Because they were winners, they were America's Team. We had to duel in the state by winning on the field, and that's what we tried to do. We knew that if we could win games, we'd get fans out.

Early Success With Houston Oilers

I was in the right situation. I was learning when I first joined the Houston Oilers. We had two or three All-Pros on defense and one hell of a teacher in Defensive Coordinator, Eddie Biles. They utilized me knowing what I could do for that defense. I could rush, I could pass-coverage, and I could do what they needed from me at my position. I had originally been a middle linebacker at Jackson State. I developed a great sense of leadership at Jackson State and carried that over into the pros.

We played as a team, as one big unit. That's what made us so successful. It wasn't just me. I had some talent, but we had a unit that played together.

Earl Campbell

Earl Campbell and I spent some time on the road as roommates. I joke with people, I slept with the best two running backs in the NFL—Earl Campbell in the pros and Walter Payton in college.

Earl would run over you, run through you, or around you. He was fast. People didn't think Earl was as fast as he was. They were both great running backs and both Pro Football Hall Of Famers.

I was lucky to play with Walter in college, and then come to the pros and play with Earl Campbell. When you practice against those guys every day, you've got to better your game and their game. The more you challenge your talent, the better you get.

Houston Oilers Players Attitude

The Houston Oilers players played hard for 60 minutes. The attitude we had was whatever it takes. We were not the type of guys who would say, "We coulda, shoulda, woulda," after a game. We wanted to win every game. We gave all we could.

I'm really proud of my career and the guys that I played with. I know that if I have to go to war, I'd love to go to war with these guys again.

Toughest Opponent

The toughest opponent for the Houston Oilers was the Pittsburgh Steelers. The challenge for us was that we knew that we needed to beat the Pittsburgh Steelers to get where we wanted to be, which was in the Super Bowl.

I still think we had a great shot in 1980. The referee made a bad call in the 1980 AFC Championship Game against the Steelers. I'll probably take that loss to my grave. I did not get my defense ready after that bad call. Sure, that was a bad call, but we still had to play defense. I feel so bad today, every time I think about that. I could not get my guys back together to play the defense we needed to win and go to the Super Bowl. You've got to get over the adversity, you've got to get over the bad calls, and you've got to play the rest of the game. We never recovered after that. I still feel some personal blame about that because we did not overcome.

Decision To Retire After Wife's Death In Car Accident

After my wife died in a car accident, I left the decision whether I should retire up to my son, who was eight at the time. Right before I went to training camp the decision of whether I should retire was in the back of my mind.

I told my son, "Daddy has to go to training camp." He said, "Dad, maybe let's go to Mobile and live with Grandma." He was referring to my mom.

I came back from training camp after the Oilers released me that year. I think the Oilers did me a favor by releasing me. I knew then what I wanted—to come into the league as an Oiler and then leave as an Oiler. It was kind of rushed, but it made it clean for me.

Photograph copyright Associates Press

Chapter 6

Kellen Winslow

College: Missouri

Career History:
San Diego Chargers (1979–1987)

1995 Inductee Pro Football Hall Of Fame

College Choice

I had a job at United Parcel Service working after school during my sophomore and junior years in high school.

One day before the end of my junior year in high school Cornelius Perry, the head football coach, along with Jimmy Lewis, an assistant coach, came to my geometry class. They told me I belonged on the football field. I'm looking at them like, "What?" I still remember being in the hallway standing next to the door of my geometry class. They took me down to the principal's office and he talked to me about the advantages of playing sports. Coach Perry told me I did things in his gym class that he'd been trying to teach other players to do. I just did it. They convinced me to come out for football.

One of the advantages of not playing football until I was in high school was that I saw other things. I came from a different perspective. My original plan was to work after school at UPS, go to a junior college, and then transfer to a four-year school.

I played on a very good high school team that had a lot of college scouts coming in from all over the country to watch us play. Scouts happened to bump into me when they watched film. My high school coaches promoted that they thought I might be okay on a college level.

Missouri, Kansas, Kansas State, and Northwestern were all recruiting me. Missouri just seemed like a good fit. The guys at Missouri did a good job of promoting how close it was to home—one hundred twenty miles away. A lot of guys at Missouri were from the St. Louis area, and it felt like a nice little family to be a part of.

Al Onofrio

Al Onofrio was the head coach when I went to Missouri. Al was a very caring man. He cared for his players and respected them. He expected them to act accordingly and always do what was best. He always said if you could pass the three-prong test in whatever you do then it's okay. The three-prong test is whatever you do reflects on your parents, your school, and the football team.

Playing Tight End At Missouri

My senior year at Missouri I had 29 or 30 catches. During the four years I was there, I had 71 catches.

Favorite Game In College

Our biggest rival was always Kansas. It's a border war—Missouri versus Kansas. Every Saturday in Columbia was special because it was such an event to have a football game. I don't remember ever playing in bad weather at a home game in Columbia. It would snow on a Monday or a Tuesday, but on Saturday just before kickoff, the sun would come out and we always had a beautiful day. We had bad weather in Nebraska and Oklahoma and places like that, but never at home during my four years.

NFL Draft

In 1979, that was the early days of ESPN. You got the information of who drafted you from the radio station or when the team called you. That was how you tracked the draft. The draft wasn't televised with all the analysis going on.

My senior year, my roommate Leo Lewis and I had moved to an area outside of Columbia into a fourplex. The night before the draft we lost phone service. I had to ride down to the local newspaper, The Columbia Tribune, to find out I was drafted.

Don Coryell

The first thing Coach Don Coryell said to me was, "How would you like to play wide receiver?" To me, that was music to my ears because most of the time that I was at Missouri, I worked out with the wide receivers. I had more fun lining up wide and running those routes than I did running in the routes the tight end did at Missouri.

Coach Coryell wasn't afraid to throw the football. He believed in throwing the ball. The goal is to score points, and the quickest way to get there is to throw it down the field. A lot of coaches, especially in the late '70s and early '80s, just feared the middle of the field. He didn't.

Advantage Of Playing Wide Receiver Before Tight End

As a wide receiver you have to get in and out of your breaks. You have to be precise with your routes. It's the person who runs the smoothest and gets in and out of the break the quickest. So, a guy who runs a 4.4, 40-yard dash may not be as good of a route runner as a guy who runs a 4.6 when the 4.6 guy is nice and smooth and precise in his routes, and understands the importance of the timing.

Learning How To Play In NFL

Learning how to play in the NFL was something more organic than taking the very direct route of taking somebody under your wing. Ernie Zampese was the receiver coach and then the offensive coordinator for the team. Al Saunders was our receiver coach. It was always, "Watch the guy." "Watch Charlie Joiner." "Watch John Jefferson." "Watch Wes Chandler." That's how you learn. The older guys taught the younger guys. It was always, "Watch, Watch" and pointing out things that the player was doing.

Dan Fouts

Dan Fouts was looking to the sideline getting the signals when people in the huddle might have been conversing. When Dan stepped in the huddle everything got quiet and all eyes were on Dan.

Depending on which team we were playing, we had a "Check with me" system that would allow Dan to get into a pass play or get into the run play or be able to check off at the line. Dan had a lot of options based on what he saw when he got under center.

Our offense got to a point where Dan learned the receivers tendencies and the receivers learned the quarterback tendencies. Dan knew where to put the ball and expected that receiver to be there. That was the beauty of our offense. It was really like a big, choreographed event for the ballet.

Setting Record For Most Catches By A Tight End In Season With 89 Catches In 1980

When I set the record for most catches in a season for a tight end, I was young and uninformed about what it meant to catch that many balls. I was just too young to understand the significance of it. At the time, all I thinking about was doing my job. The great thing about playing for the Chargers was I was just a piece of the offense. I wasn't the one who had to carry the load. There w/ould be a week where I would catch two or three passes, and a week I would catch five or six passes. It was up to the quarterback to take what the defense gave us. The year I had 89 catches, John Jefferson had 82 catches and Charlie Joiner had 71 catches. That was unheard of at that time. We had running backs that had 24, 26, and 29 catches in Chuck Muncie, Clarence Williams, and Mike Thomas. That was the beauty of the offense.

A coach like Don Coryell understood the personnel and didn't get caught up in certain parameters on players. He was a coach who watched a player and the things the player did during practice and allowed the player to take advantage of those things during games. Coach Coryell put in the tight end option pass because he saw that I would stay out after practice and play catch with the wide receivers. He said, "Let's put this in. Let's use this skill."

The same thing with James Brooks who was probably pound for pound one of the better players in the National Football League at the time.

Tying NFL Record For Most Touchdown Receptions In A Game

The game against the Oakland Raiders was a must win for us. We had started off the season strong and then ran into a mid season rut. We needed the victory against Oakland. Had we lost that game in Oakland, we probably would have been eliminated from the playoffs. We were playing the Raiders up there and we had to win. We got into the game and things just started to flow. The Raiders liked to play man-to-man. They liked to rush four players and thought they could pressure opposing teams. Dan Fouts did a great job of taking advantage of the mismatches.

They could have double-teamed me, but they had to pick their poison. Did they want Wes Chandler or John Jefferson with the ball in the middle of the field running if they double-teamed me? Did they want Charlie Joiner to run a quick route on them and make one of their defensive players miss Charlie and he gets into the end zone? Do they want the ball in the hands of Chuck Muncie? Did they want that ball in the hands of James Brooks? They figured they would make me [the big, slow guy] beat them.

"The Epic In Miami" 1982 Playoff Game San Diego Chargers vs. Miami Dolphins

It was a hot day in Miami during the 1982 playoff game against the Miami Dolphins. Everybody was playing under the same conditions.

There are so many things that I remember about that game. We were using zoom, zip, slide—all kinds of motion—and I was the motion guy, so that took a toll on me. Then Miami got a little physical with me. Being a playoff game you've got all the injuries and issues that you've dealt with during the year that come into play. I thought I prepared myself properly for the weather conditions including the humidity, but it just all took a toll on me. We realized that we couldn't continue this type of motion on offense. The Chargers coaches took some of the burden off of me and used other players in motion, or in some cases, went away from it.

I think we were 17-0 when I went to the sideline, and Charlie Joiner was sitting on the bench while the whole Chargers team was celebrating. I think it was right after Wes Chandler had scored on a punt return for us. Charlie's sitting there, and he's got this long look on his face. I thought he was hurt so I go over to check on him.

Charlie being the veteran that he was said to me, "We're too high. We're too excited." I said, "What do you mean?" I will never forget what he said.

"You don't come into Miami and do this to a Don Shula football team." He said, "Don is going to pull David Woodley. He's going to put in Don Strock. Don's going to throw the football and we're going to be here all day." The very next series, Coach Shula pulled Woodley, the rookie out of LSU, and put in Don Strock, the veteran gunslinger. We were there the rest of the day. I never will forget that.

I got upset when Charlie told me that because I could not see myself being a part of a team that had that big of a lead and then lost it. So whenever I came out the game, I was trying to get back into the game.

The decision to put me in on special teams was planned. The special team was the do-or-die team. We needed to play to win. We put the best people in on special teams to do the job. It didn't matter what position they played, what their salary was, or what their profile was, because we needed to win the game. So, I was on the do-or-die field goal block team. My job was to try to time the Dolphins field goal kick up, leap over the middle, and block the kick.

I remember getting in the huddle with Leroy Jones, Louie Kelcher, Fred Dean, and Gary Johnson. They were looking at me and I was looking at them. I said, "Okay guys, just give me some penetration and I'm going to get it. I'll get it."

I was just trying to talk it up and really felt that we could block the field goal. It just so happened that we got some penetration and I timed the kick just right and the ball hit my finger. I didn't knock it down. It wasn't manly where I slapped the ball to the ground. The ball just hit my finger, which took a few rotations off the ball and made the kick come up short.

1982 AFC Championship Game San Diego Chargers vs. Cincinnati Bengals

We found out afterward that there was some discussion about whether the 1982 AFC Championship Game should be played or not. Urban legend is that the NFL called a cold weather expert in Chicago and asked if the players would be okay. I'm sure the cold weather expert was sitting in his den next to the fireplace with a blanket over him and a dog lying across his feet as he said, "Oh, yeah, they'll be okay if they just dress properly." That's my version of it.

The wind chill factor was 59 below. The ball was a rock. The field was a rock. Our thigh pads were a rock. Our helmet was a rock. Everything just froze.

They would not cancel that game today. Today they have cold weather equipment. We were making our equipment up. We got our ankles taped, then put on a sock, then put a plastic bag over our foot, then put on another sock, and then put on our shoe. The bag was there to keep the cold air from getting to the sweat on your feet so you wouldn't get frostbite.

I wore two pairs of gloves. One was a pair of baseball batting gloves, and the other pair was a pair of scuba diving gloves that were cut down as small as possible. There was no Under Armour® in those days. We might have been okay with the Under Armour® cold weather body suit. We wore either pantyhose or thermal underwear.

That day we used the same offensive game plan what we had been using all year. We tried to make some adjustments in the passing game by going to a shorter passing game and running the ball. We had Chuck Muncie at running back. But I have to give the Bengals credit. They did a better job adjusting to the weather and were able to put a bunch of points up. I remember the first pass that Dan Fouts threw. The wind just took it and blew it away.

Not Playing In A Super Bowl

We played in two consecutive AFC Championship Games; one was against the Cincinnati Bengals and the year before against the Oakland Raiders. We thought that we had as good a chance as anybody of playing in the Super Bowl. We just came up short twice.

The Raiders got a very fortuitous bounce early in the AFC Championship Game in San Diego. The ball got tipped and went right into Raymond Chester's hands. He ran to the end zone for the touchdown. We ended up losing by seven points.

The next season in the playoffs, after playing in Miami against the Dolphins and winning, we ended up in Cincinnati playing against the Bengals in one of the coldest games in NFL history.

Ability To Line Up In Any Formation

It wasn't like I was so unique in being able to line up in different formations. There were other players in the league who had the same ability—Charlie Sanders in Detroit, John Mackey did similar things in the earlier days of the tight end, and Jackie Smith with the Cardinals was a great athlete.

It was Don Coryell who said, "Let's use Kellen this way." He trusted me with the offense and knowing the different concepts, understanding the concepts, and playing the different roles. Then he just moved me around. He gave me the ability to do that. There were other guys who could have done that before me and during the time I was playing, but a lot of coaches just didn't have the innovation to do it.

Decision To Retire

When the moment of fire is burning and people give you a chance, you want to be out there. There's a fire that burns inside every player. If you're honest with yourself, you know when that fire starts to diminish and it's time to do something else. It was time for me to go do something else. The team had changed. I had gone from being one of the youngest on the team to one of the oldest. Dan Fouts, Charlie Joiner, Wes Chandler, Billy Shields, and Rolf Benirschke were all gone. I think Donnie Macek, Dennis McKnight, and I were the only ones that were left.

Pro Football Hall Of Fame Induction
I still can't believe I am in the Pro Football Hall Of Fame. I go to the Hall and they treat me so well, with so much reverence. I almost didn't play football in high school. One decision changed my entire life. I was very close to deciding to not play football.

Everywhere I played, I was so fortunate. I played on a great high school football team and because of that, schools came around looking for guys and they bumped into me.

I played on a great college football team. We were loaded. I played with James Wilder, Earl Gant, Gerry Ellis, Leo Lewis, and Eric Wright. We were turning out guys who played in the pros on offensive, defensive line, etc. I fit in at the right time.

Then I was picked in the NFL Draft and end up in San Diego. I was the final piece of the puzzle for the offense. It's been a very blessed, very fortunate, situation for me. That's why I'm in the Pro Football Hall Of Fame. If I had played with another team at that time, you wouldn't be talking to me.

Keys To Being Successful In Football & Life
You can't have a low IQ or not understand the concepts and play football well. You just can't. I tell people that all the time.

I played chess in high school. I lettered in chess for three years and football in one. One day I realized that football and chess were a lot alike. I thought, "Oh, I get football now. I know what I do. Better yet, I know why I do it and I know what everybody else does. I know why they do it. Football just made sense to me."

Some people think that because you play in the NFL, that you're not very bright. There are many former players who have gone off and become professionals—doctors, lawyers, very successful people—or become leaders, and football was the basis for that. I just get so upset when I hear those stereotypical type things.

Jim Brown
It's so hard to compare players across decades, eras, world changes, etc. Jim was so much better than everybody else. He was bigger, stronger, and faster. He was playing a position where he had the ball the majority of the time, so his impact was always great.

You have to look at it by era to see who was the superior player during that era, because it changes by era. Jim was a big running back. Now every team has a big running back or two huge running backs. I was one of the bigger tight ends in the League when I played at 6'-5", 245-250 lbs. I'm the H-back in today's game. You've got guys who are 6'-6", 265-270 pounds, playing tight end and running legitimate 4.6 40s. That barroom talk about which guy was the greatest of all time … I just kind of let it go in one ear and out the other. I really appreciate a player for the way they played and the things that they did when they played. Jim Brown was just so much better than everybody else it was just ridiculous.

Chuck Muncie

Chuck Muncie was so amazing. He was a great basketball player. He could jump out of the gym. He could have been anything he wanted to be. When Chuck came to us in San Diego, we were like, "Oh, wow, he can't be that big. He's just huge."

The coaching staff understood what they had and his ability. When he came to play, there was nobody better.

In one game against the Denver Broncos, I was the basically the fullback and Chuck was the tailback. So you're talking about a 250-pound tight end/fullback, and a 248-pound tailback in Chuck. We would line up in the I formation, which is physically daunting. Then we would go in motion, and run a play based on what Dan Fouts saw and how Denver reacted to the motion. We lost that game.

Two or three weeks later we played Denver again, and we changed the strategy where we lined up in the I formation and snapped the ball. Denver was waiting for us to make the adjustment, and we snapped the ball and caught them off guard. To me that was brilliant coaching.

When Chuck would get the ball and I was leading as the fullback, I wanted to get out of his way. I didn't want Chuck running up behind me or over me, because he would. So I was really moving and finding somebody to put a helmet on. The defensive back or linebacker was looking for you because they didn't want to run up against Chuck. He was so much fun to watch. He could catch the ball coming out of the backfield. He could run over you, run away from you, and make you miss. He had great vision.

San Diego Charger Kellen Winslow is helped off the field by teammates following the Chargers win over the Miami Dolphins on January 2, 1982 in the AFC Divisional Playoff Game.
Photograph copyright Associated Press

Chapter 7

Kenny Easley

College: UCLA Career History: Seattle Seahawks (1981-1987) 2017 Inductee Pro Football Hall Of Fame

College Choice

My choice of which college to attend came down between Michigan and UCLA. I really liked Michigan when I went there. I was impressed with not only their athletic program, but that they had a 100,000-seat stadium. I could not believe that 100,000 people would attend a football game, week after week after week. That was unbelievable to me. I just liked the way they ran their program there. I mean, they have a long history of success, so I sort of got locked into that opportunity. Michigan was going to give me an opportunity to play for a championship team. The problem was that they wanted me to play quarterback. I played quarterback and free safety in high school. Most of the teams that recruited me were viewing me as a quarterback, with the notable exception of UCLA.

UCLA want me to play free safety, and I wanted to play free safety. When I told Bo Schembechler that I didn't want to play quarterback, he was taken aback. He said, "You have to be kidding me. Why would you want to play free safety when you can play quarterback at the greatest football institution in the nation?" I told him that I really thought I was just a good athlete playing quarterback, but I thought I could really be a fantastic free safety. He just wouldn't buy into that. When he left my house, he was really upset with me and the fact that I didn't have enough sense to take advantage of an opportunity that only a few had a chance at. Conversely, UCLA wanted me as a free safety, so that sort of sealed the deal.

The fact that Michigan quarterbacks traditionally handed the ball off to the running backs for the majority of plays was a consideration. My dad and I talked about that. At that particular time there wasn't a plethora of black quarterbacks in the National Football League. It was sort of just coming into vogue at that particular time in college football.

Most black quarterbacks were option quarterbacks not throwing quarterbacks. We thought about all that. I knew that to make it in the NFL, you had to be a throwing quarterback.

Being an option quarterback at the University of Michigan or anywhere else was not going to get me to my objective, which was to play in the National Football League.

Terry Donahue

The interesting thing about Terry Donahue, and he'll tell you this himself, is that when I got to UCLA in 1977, that was his first season as head coach. He had to go through a learning process. Because it was his first season, I think he sort of overreacted when it came to disciplining the players. He'll tell you that today. We really didn't get along famously when I was there because he thought that I was too much of a hothead, or I wasn't coachable, and so forth. We bumped heads a great deal the first couple of years.

I believe it was during my junior year when he kicked me off the team. J.D. Morgan, the athletic director, overrode Terry's decision. J.D. said, "We brought this kid out here 3,000 miles from home, and we're not just going to kick him off the team for what he did." I had hit the quarterback who had a red jersey on. J.D. Morgan came to my defense and said, "You know, the kid is 18. He made a mistake. You just can't kick him off the team for doing something like that."

Coach Donahue had recruited me and signed me to come to UCLA. Luckily cooler heads prevailed and after a couple of days or maybe even a week, Coach Donahue, through the defensive coordinator, told me to come back on the football team.

Terry and I had sort of a rocky relationship. I spoke to him after I found out I made the Pro Football Hall of Fame. That was the first time I had spoken to him since I left UCLA in 1981. He called and we talked passionately. It was good to talk to him and hash out those things that had bothered our relationship 30 years ago.

College

I got an opportunity to play right off the bat at UCLA. When I got there in 1977, a senior free safety named Michael Coulter was number one on the depth chart. A junior by the name of Johnny Lynn was at number two. Then in our freshman class, we had two freshman free safeties, Dave Gomer and me. I had a big mountain to climb. I came to UCLA on a mission because there were so many people in Virginia and from my high school that didn't think that I could do it. So, I was sort of on a mission to show them that they were wrong.

The first game of the season we played the Houston Cougars in the Astrodome, in Houston. The defensive coordinator played Michael Coulter the first two quarters of the first half, and I played the two quarters of the second half. Michael Coulter never started another game. I didn't find it easy. It was hard work. I believe I had seven interceptions and led the conference as defensive freshman player of the year. I was just on my way from there. I just got better. We had a coaching change on defense, and then they brought in Gary Rikeny as the defensive back coach. I learned a great deal from him. By my senior year, they brought in Tom Hays. I also learned a great deal from him. I was very fortunate. I got some good coaching there, but I was also a hard worker.

Playing Basketball At UCLA

Basketball was good conditioning for me. I was discovered playing intramural basketball at UCLA. The UCLA junior varsity basketball coach asked me to come out for the junior varsity team. I was running and getting the benefit of exercising by playing basketball, which is good conditioning for a football player. I had a great time playing basketball at UCLA. I led the junior varsity team in scoring.

Comparing Football To Basketball At UCLA

Basketball was the dominant sport at UCLA, even then. John Wooden had retired the year before I got to

UCLA, but basketball was still the cream of the sports there. Terry Donahue was in his first year as head coach during my freshman year. Coach Donahue went on to have some really successful football teams in the '80s with Troy Aikman and all of the other players that came along. Basketball was key.

Best Game Played At UCLA

I don't think I had a best game. I was fairly consistent all the way through college because of the way I played. I went out with the intention of playing every game the best that I could play, because I was uniquely aware that any one of those games could have been my last game. So if any game was going to be my last game, I wanted people to be able to say that the last game I played was my best game.

That's the way I played every game. Some players can view a particular game and say, "That was my best game." I can't say that because I played every game as if it was going to be my last game.

NFL Draft

The day before the draft, San Francisco 49ers Head Coach Bill Walsh and his entire defensive staff asked me to meet him and the coaches in Pauley Pavilion. They came down to UCLA and worked me out. After working out I took a shower and came back out to talk to them. Bill and his defensive staff were sitting about 10 rows up in the stands. I sat down and Bill said, "Hey, look, we have the 8th pick in the first round tomorrow. If we select you with the 8th pick, would you be okay with that?" I said, "Absolutely," and we did a little bit more talking.

I asked him if he would play me at free safety and he said he would. I knew that they had Dwight Hicks playing free safety for them.

I remember I first met Dwight Hicks at Michigan, when I went there for a recruitment visit in 1977. I had a great deal of respect for the work that Dwight Hicks had done at Michigan and the work he was doing for the 49ers at free safety. I was concerned about that. I wanted to know, if they drafted me, what they were going to do with me. He said right away, "Yeah, we're going to play you there. We'll figure out what we'll do with Dwight Hicks," so that's where I thought I was going.

I actually called a few people, including my mom, and told them there was a pretty good chance I was going to get drafted by San Francisco the next day. My mom didn't like that because that just drew me further from home.

I told a couple of my buddies that I was going to San Francisco. When Seattle drafted me, I was really upset and thought about telling Leigh Steinberg, my agent, to engineer a trade. When I went to Seattle the day of the draft, I was really taken by the acceptance of the fans. It seemed like the fans were really excited to have me there and have me as a part of the team. So, I decided to forgo any type of trade and go play for the Seattle Seahawk fans.

I absolutely don't regret it because Seattle has the best fans in the National Football League. That was evident some 30 years ago when they wanted me to be a part of their organization.

Jack Patera

Jack Patera was a different guy. First of all, when I got to Seattle in 1981, the organization was only five years old and the team was still trying to find its way. Seattle didn't have a great deal of talent. They had Jim Zorn and Steve Largent on offense. Those two guys were sort of the offensive show. They were still trying to build a defense.

I give Jack Patera a great deal of credit because before I got there, they drafted Manu Tuiasosopo in 1979 as their first round draft pick. Then in 1980, they drafted Jacob Green, a defensive end out of Texas A&M as their first round pick. In 1981, they drafted me as their first round pick and in 1982, they drafted another defensive player, Jeff Bryant, as their first round pick. So, they were really working on building a defense.

Jack was definitely trying to build the defense, but he got fired about two or three years after I got to Seattle. Jack had a tough job because he was the first coach of the Seahawks. It was tough sledding for him.

Chuck Knox

Chuck Knox was named head coach in 1983, and brought in a bunch of veteran players including Reggie Mackenzie, Terry Jackson, Charle Young, and Cullen Bryant. Being a young team those guys came in and basically taught us how to win and how to play pro football.

We started winning right away. Chuck got to Seattle in 1983, and the very first year we went to the AFC Championship Game. We lost to the Raiders, who ended up beating the Washington Redskins in the Super Bowl that year. We had beaten the Raiders twice during the regular season in 1983. We beat them in Los Angeles, and then we beat them in Seattle. Then in 1984, we went 12 and 4 and played the Miami Dolphins again in the first round of the playoffs. We had beaten them the year before. We lost to them that time.

Playing Strong Safety After Being Drafted By Seahawks

Jack Patera took a look at me and probably thought that I was a run stopping defensive back, so he put me at strong safety even though I had played free safety basically all of my life. From the time I was in Pop Warner football, I played free safety. I played free safety in middle school, I played free safety in high school, and I obviously played free safety at UCLA, but when I got to Seattle, they put me at strong safety.

I should have demanded that I play free safety. I think I had the right to do that as a first round draft pick. I grew up in an environment where when you were asked to do something, you learned how to do it and did it. So when they asked me to play strong safety, instead of bucking the system and saying, "I want to play free safety," I just did it. That was the type of environment that I grew up in. Although I regret not telling them I wanted to play free safety, I did what they wanted me to do and tried to make the best of it.

Tom Catlin

In 1983, Seattle hired Tom Catlin as defensive coordinator. He revamped our defense and put me in position to make plays on defense. He took advantage of my athletic ability and designed our defense to take advantage of what I did best, which was run, hit, and make plays.

We went from a two high safety defense to a single free safety. He always put me in a position where I had a chance to affect the offense. So I have to thank Tom Catlin for having the wisdom to take advantage of the things that I did best.

Playing Philosophy

The only way I knew how to play was to just lay it out there every game. If I got hurt, so be it. If I never played again, that's the nature of the beast, but I was going to play. I was going to play as if it was going to be my last game, and in hindsight I don't regret that. I believe that because I played that way, I was looked at again as a Pro Football Hall Of Famer when I was in the Senior Division. I think the voters looked at the way that I played during my seven years of playing, and thought that they had to consider me as a Hall Of Fame player. I was NFL Defensive Player Of the Year, AFC rookie of the year, made Pro Bowls, I was an All Pro, and I was named to the All Decade Team of the '80s. Maybe the way I played was special enough for the voters to have reconsidered me for the Pro Football Hall Of Fame.

1984 Game Against Kansas City Chiefs

Our game against the Kansas City Chiefs in 1984 was a game for the ages. We had six interceptions in that game and returned four of them for touchdowns, setting an NFL record for interceptions for touchdowns in a game. From a player's perspective, it wasn't much of a game because we dominated the game. I believe we beat them 45-0, so it wasn't one of our harder games. It turned into a cakewalk of a game.

Those are the games that you like to play because once you get up by a certain amount of points; the opposing team has to throw on almost every down. When we got up by 30 points, Kansas City threw the football on every play after that. All we had to do as defenders was jump every route. A defender is probably going to make an interception at some point if they're jumping every route. The only reason you would jump every route is if you're 30 points ahead and you know that the opposing team is going to have to throw. It's going to increase your chances of making interceptions.

I've played in better and more interesting games, but certainly when your team gets six interceptions and four of them are returned for interceptions, it's a big joy that you can produce those results.

Seattle Seahawks Defense

Our entire defensive line was the catalyst of our defense. The defensive line consisted of Jacob Green, Jeff Bryant, and Joe Nash. Those guys put a great deal of pressure on the quarterback, which made my job in the secondary a whole lot easier. When a quarterback is being pressured all the time, he's going to throw interceptions. In 1984 we had 38 interceptions and 60 turnovers, finishing second behind the Chicago Bears, who led the league that year in turnovers. The guys who set the table for the rest of the defense were Jacob Green, Joe Nash, and Jeff Bryant.

Practicing Against Steve Largent

I hardly ever practiced against Steve Largent unless it was during the off-season. During the season, our number two defense practiced against our number one offense, and our number two offense practiced against our number one defense. I hardly ever got a chance to practice against Steve because of the way that our practice was set up.

During the off-season when Steve and I were working against each other, I tried to cover him as many times as I could, as would the rest of the defensive backs. We knew that Steve was going to make us better covering him. In a two-hour workout, I probably got a chance to cover him 8 to 10 times in between the rest of the defensive backs who wanted to cover him.

We had other good receivers too. Obviously none better than Steve, but they were quality NFL receivers. So if you ended up covering say Paul Johns, Steve Raible, or Ray Butler you were going to get some good work in. There's no question that Steve was the best receiver we had, and when you got a chance to cover him, you knew you were covering the best.

1987 NFL Players Strike
We had a couple of our veteran players on the Seattle Seahawks that crossed the players' picket line. That was really the hardest part of the strike because the players that crossed the picket line were out there playing with the replacement players when the league got up running again with the replacement players. To see our teammates out there playing was really difficult on us. It was a tough time for the NFL and for the players who hung in there, staying out until the strike was resolved. It took some teams longer than others to resolve those types of issues. Those issues were resolved, at least on our team. We got back to playing and being respectful of our teammates.

Discovering I Had A Kidney Ailment In 1988
Discovering I had a kidney ailment was one of the toughest things that I had to deal with, not only during my career, but also in life. I was 28 years old and at the top of my game when I found out that I had a kidney ailment. More importantly, I found out much later, once I sued the Seahawks, that the organization knew about my ailment. The Seahawks were trying to unload me, hoping that the team they traded me to would miss finding out that I had a kidney ailment.

The Arizona Cardinals traded for me and I failed their physical. The media found out that it was a kidney ailment and the Seahawks general manager said, "Whatever ailment caused Kenny to fail his physical, it was non-football related." I just could not believe that he would make a statement like that. At that point it wasn't clear what had caused the problem, but once my lawyers subpoenaed all of my records from 1981 thru 1987, we found out that the organization knew about the kidney ailment and they were going to try to make me someone else's problem.

It was really disheartening that the team I had played for, and played so well for, would do that to me. After that, I sort of divorced myself from the team for well over 15 years. It wasn't until 2002 that I ever talked to anyone in the Seattle organization. That was when they wanted to place me in the Seattle Ring Of Honor. During the time I was away from the organization, Paul Allen had purchased the team from Ken Behring who had bought the team from the Nordstrom family.

Being Inducted Into the Seattle Seahawks Ring Of Honor
First of all, I felt like I should have been in the Seattle Seahawks Ring Of Honor already. Secondly, I was grateful to Paul Allen and the organization for reaching out to me and bringing me back into the Seahawks family. I thought that it was long overdue. I had been away from the team for 15 years with no communication. That was when Garry Wright, who was vice president of the team at the time, called me. He told me that Mr. Allen said they couldn't induct anyone else into the Seahawk Ring Of Honor until we induct Kenny Easley.

It made sense for me to drop the animosity and do the right thing after a 15-year absence. Plus, I had young children, my youngest being 6, and they had never seen me play pro football. It made sense at that time to drop the animosity and go in the Ring Of Honor. It gave my children a chance to understand that their dad had played pro football and had done it well.

Pro Football Hall Of Fame Induction
The Pro Football Hall Of Fame voters decided to take a fresh look at my career, thanks to Frank Cooney and Bob Kaupang. Bob was sending articles to the Pro Football Hall Of Fame about my career

and the things that I had done. The voters decided to take a fresh look and thought, perhaps we need to get away from the criteria that a guy had to play double digit years to be considered for the Hall Of Fame."

When you look at the Hall Of Fame, you have Gale Sayers who played six years, and my former defensive back coach, Jack Christianson who I believe played eight or nine years. The voters probably thought they needed to take a look at the quality of the years rather than the quantity of the years.

I believe with Terrell Davis and me, getting in with seven years of service each, and you can also include Kurt Warner because I believe he played just eight years in the NFL, hopefully what happened this year will dispel the myth that you have to play double digit years to even be considered a Hall Of Fame type player.

It's going to sound interesting or strange, but it was like Christmas for me when David Baker, President of the Pro Football Hall Of Fame, knocked on my hotel room door and told me I had been selected for the Hall Of Fame. It was like being a little kid again. You go to bed the night before Christmas knowing it's Christmas Eve, knowing that Santa Claus is going to come sometime during the night. That's what it was like having David Baker knock on my door. When David knocked, I was excited to open the door. Then he announced that I was a Hall Of Famer. After that it was like Christmas when you get to play with your toys.

That's how it felt to me, and it may not be an apt description, but that's the only way that I can explain it because when I opened that door and it was David Baker, man, was I excited. My family was excited. I had my wife and children there, and they got to yelling, hugging me, and being excited with tears running down their faces. It's just something that is hard to describe to someone who has not experienced it, that type of joy.

Seattle Seahawk Kenny Easley knocks New York Jet quarterback Richard Todd to the ground.
Photograph copyright Associated Press

Chapter 8

Russ Grimm

```
College:
Pittsburgh

Career History:
As Player:
Washington Redskins (1981-1991)

As Coach:
Washington Redskins (1992-2000)
Pittsburgh Steelers (2001-2006)
Arizona Cardinals (2007-2012)
Tennessee Titans (2016-2017)

2010 Inductee Pro Football Hall Of Fame
```

College Choice
I actually attended the University of Pittsburgh by default. I wanted to be a linebacker at Penn State. Penn State was recruiting me early on. Once the recruiting period hit, I didn't hear from them for about two or three weeks. They came in late and I had already made up my mind that I was going to stay in the area where I lived and go to Pittsburgh.

College
My first two years at Pittsburgh I was a linebacker. I played on special teams some of my sophomore year. Head Coach Jackie Sherrill called me into his office after my sophomore year, right before spring ball, and said that they had lost a bunch of guys on the offensive line. They thought it was in my best interest if I switched over and played center.

I never had my hand in a three-point stance prior to Coach Sherrill asking me to play center. I was a linebacker and quarterback in high school. Playing center was new to me. I weighed 242 pounds at the time, and spring ball was a little rough because we had an All- American nose tackle in Dave Logan, who went on to play for the Tampa Bay Buccaneers. I came back in the fall weighing 265 pounds and won a starting job. By my senior year, I weighed about 280 pounds.

I think we finished second in the country in both 1979 and 1980. Nobody wanted to play us. Any team ranked number 1 didn't want to play us in a bowl game. We always had to sit and hope somebody lost and they didn't lose. That's the way it goes sometimes. We had some really good football teams.

Joe Moore
Joe Moore, our offensive line coach at Pittsburgh, was great. He's a great motivator and a good teacher. We had a lot of good players. All five guys that I played with on the offensive line during my senior year all went on to play in the NFL. Mark May was our right tackle and Jimbo Covert was our left tackle.

Not Winning A National Championship At Pittsburgh
It was tough not winning a National Championship at Pittsburgh because we felt we had the best team. We lost one game each year. We lost one game to North Carolina 17-7. During my senior year, we lost to Florida State 36-22. We should have run the table.

Dan Marino
It was great playing with Dan Marino at Pittsburgh. The guy was talented. He got the ball out of his hand in a hurry. It was a lot of fun. There were a lot of games that were over by halftime.

NFL Draft
I thought I had a chance to play in the NFL after my junior year. I was just glad with whoever drafted me. The draft wasn't televised back then. Actually, it was trout season and I was fishing that morning. When I got home, my parents said the Redskins had called. I called them back and they said they'd drafted me. I was off to D.C.

Early Years With Redskins
We started out the 1981 season 0-5. We finished 1981, 8-8. We thought that things had turned for the better. We had a little momentum going. We won the Super Bowl after the 1982 season. In 1983, we went to the Super Bowl again, but we lost to the Raiders. We had some good teams.

1982 & 1983 Washington Redskins
The key to winning Super Bowl XVII against the Miami Dolphins after the 1982 season was Head Coach Joe Gibbs staying with the game plan of running the ball.

In 1982 and 1983, we were solid everywhere including special teams. The 1983 team has a record. We were plus 42 or 43 in turnover ratio. I don't think that will ever be broken. We were just a smart and physical football team. We tried not to beat ourselves.

Prefer Run Blocking Or Pass Blocking
I preferred run blocking. Pass blocking is a little passive. You've got to be under control for a little while. I always say it's like controlled aggression. Run blocking, you can cut loose.

"The Hogs"
Our Offensive Line Coach, Joe Bugel, gave us "The Hogs" nickname. During training camp Coach Bugel said, "Let's just go hogs, time to hit the sleds." One of the reporters picked up on it. The next thing you know, the fans got a hold of it and it took off from there.

The nickname was great. We had our own fan base and things like that. Then again, every Sunday we had to be able to back it up.

Super Bowl XVIII Washington Redskins vs. Los Angeles Raiders
We played the Los Angeles Raiders that year and beat them. It was a tight game and we beat them in the last minute or two of the game. They were a good football team. They were solid and talented.

We made some mistakes during Super Bowl XVIII. Joe Theismann threw an interception on a screen for a Raider touchdown. The Raiders had some big plays on special teams against us. We may have gotten a little complacent too, since we had already beaten them during the year.

Toughest Defensive Lineman Played Against
The toughest defensive lineman I played against my first couple of years in the NFL was Randy White of the Dallas Cowboys. He was quick and strong. He had both those qualities as a defensive lineman. And, he was a good player.

Darryl Grant
I went against usually Darryl Grant in practice. He was physical and quick. We wanted to make each other better. You can't just take plays off and go easy. Nobody gets better then.

Joe Bugel
Joe Bugel was a great teacher of assignments. I think that was his biggest thing. Our offensive linemen went into games knowing exactly whom we were going against and what we needed to do against them. We never went in where the defensive linemen surprised us with something. Coach Bugel was solid in making sure we knew whom we were covering and we knew exactly what to do.

Washington Redskins Winning Three Super Bowls With Three Different Starting Quarterbacks
All three of those teams weren't one-dimensional. We didn't necessarily need the quarterback to carry us. We had a running game. We had a defense. It was a combination of everything.

Washington Redskins Fans
Washington, D.C. is a transient area. As long as the Washington Redskins are playing well, everybody jumps on the bandwagon. As soon as things start to head downhill [for the team] for a week or two, everybody jumps back, and says, "I'm originally from Boston.

I'm originally from Pittsburgh. I'm originally from wherever." They jump back to their home team if the Redskins are not playing well. I loved the fans in D.C. They were great.

Head Coach Joe Gibbs
Head Coach Joe Gibbs was a hard worker and consistent. We knew he slept at the office. He put in the time. When he installed the game plan, we could look at it and know that all the 'i's were dotted, the 't's were crossed, and everything was checked off.

Leader Of The Offensive Line
I don't know if the offensive line really had any leaders. It was more making sure everybody was on the same page. The guys that were playing on our offensive line just fit that mold. We were a close- knit group that didn't want to let the other guys down.

Favorite Washington Redskins Team Played On
I would say probably the 1982 team was my favorite Washington Redskins team I played on, because it was my second year in the NFL and my first Super Bowl win. I tell people all the time that the 1983 team may have been the best team that I ever played on. We lost two games that year, both of them by one point. Then we lost the Super Bowl.

Pro Football Hall Of Fame Induction
When I played, I never thought about being inducted into the Pro Football Hall of Fame. It was never a big thing on my mind. It was never a big goal. I just wanted to win games.

When I was done playing, it was something that I looked forward to. When I made it, I couldn't believe I made the Hall of Fame. Then I went to Canton. I was in the same room as and listening to Joe Greene, Franco Harris, and other guys that have been in the Hall Of Fame a long, long time, talking about their experiences. It was a great feeling.

Joe Jacoby
Joe Jacoby deserves to be in the Pro Football Hall Of Fame. It's especially tough for offensive linemen because there really aren't any stats on them. It's not like the defensive linemen, where you can count how many sacks they had or anything like that. One time, I told the Pro Football Hall Of Fame Selectors if they don't induct seven guys a year, then there's going to be a lot of guys not getting in that deserve to be in.

Favorite Players Growing Up
Growing up I always wanting to be the next Dick Butkus. I was also a big Jack Lambert fan, since I grew up in the Pittsburgh area. I just liked to hit people. I wanted to be a linebacker. I started out as a linebacker my first two years at the University of Pittsburgh. Then the coaches switched me over to the offensive line and I had to put my hand in the dirt.

Harry Carson
Harry Carson, with the New York Giants, and I used to have some battles. There would be days that I thought, I got him now; he's going to go out of the game. He wouldn't leave the field, though. He was a tough nut.

Coaching Philosophy
I tell the players I coach, "I'm not going to get up here and try to have you do something that I know can't be done." I think the players all know I've played. I treat them the way I wanted to be treated. They play pretty well.

Comparing Linemen From Different Eras To Today's Linemen
Somebody wanted me to compare myself to Alan Faneca when I was coaching him with the Pittsburgh Steelers. I said, "It's not even close. Alan is 30 pounds heavier than I was. He's quicker than I was. He's stronger than I was."

Everybody thought that we had the biggest offensive line in the league when I played for the Redskins. We had one guy over 300 in Joe Jacoby when we got the nickname "Hogs." We were the biggest line in the league. I can't remember any time in the last 20 years of my coaching, that I had a guy weigh less than 300 pounds.

Favorite Games
I had a lot of favorite games. The runs John Riggins had in the Super Bowl against Miami; the big second quarter we had against the Denver Broncos in the Super Bowl ... There are certain moments here and there. After awhile, it all blends together.

Super Bowl XXII Washington Redskins vs. Denver Broncos
Super Bowl XXII was great. I tell people all the time that Jay Schroeder won 11 games for us that year. Then Jay got hurt and Doug Williams stepped in. Doug was hot. We just stayed with Doug through the playoffs.

George Rogers was our running back all the way to the Super Bowl. Then Coach Gibbs says we're going to start Timmy Smith in the Super Bowl. We're looking around going, what? Timmy runs for 200 some yards; a Super Bowl record back then. You just never know. Those are coach's decisions. Things panned out. I guess that was a good call.

New York Giant Lawrence Taylor tries to evade the Redskins Russ Grimm. Photograph copyright Associated Press

Chapter 9

Mike Munchak

College:
Penn State

Career History:
Houston Oilers (1982-1993)

Coaching History:
Houston Oilers (1994–1996) (Offensive assistant/quality control coach)
Tennessee Oilers/Titans (1997–2010) (Offensive line coach)
Tennessee Titans (2011–2013) (Head coach)
Pittsburgh Steelers (2014–Present) (Offensive line coach)

2001 Inductee Pro Football Hall Of Fame

<u>College Choice</u>
I was probably a middle of the road recruit. People thought Penn State was where I always wanted to go. It really wasn't. I knew of Penn State, obviously. I knew of Coach Joe Paterno and of his great reputation. I didn't know where I wanted to go, or what the future held for me. To be honest, even when I was in high school, I'm one of those guys who just enjoyed the moment.

My junior year I started getting hand-sealed letters of interest from coaches in me playing football for them in college.

I think that's when it hit me [the end of my junior year] that I had an opportunity to maybe get a scholarship to continue in football. I was one of those tweener guys. Because of my height and weight at the time it wasn't an obvious thing, what position I'd be playing in college.

My senior year, I heard from Penn State and some other teams. I took my five or six visits. My sister was going to Penn State at the time. Penn State was only a couple hours away from home. I went for a visit to Penn State. One of the assistant coaches had called me to set up a visit. I went out there in January of my senior year in high school for a visit.

That's when I first met Coach Paterno. It was during a dinner when they had all the recruits in town. There were 15-20 guys there. We were there for the weekend in order to get a feel for what Penn State was like. It's really different than most visits when you would only go for one night.

At the time, there was no football dorm at Penn State. The players were spread around the campus like the regular students. Players were in normal dorm rooms.

At Penn State you stayed in a dorm room as a recruit. You slept on a cot in a room with two Penn State football players. Coach Paterno wanted recruits to experience what they were getting themselves into if they went to Penn State.

That was unique because most schools I visited I stayed in a hotel, which had a nice setup. Whereas at Penn State, it was, "This is what we're all about, here's how we do business, and here's what you can expect." I got a real good taste of college life, for what it was going to be like in the dorms with not just football players.

I thought that was kind of interesting. I actually liked that way of recruiting. I got a chance to spend time with the players and assistant coaches.

On Sunday before I left, I had a chance to sit down with Coach Paterno. That was my first face-to-face meeting with him. Obviously, I was scared to death for that meeting. I was an 18-year-old boy talking to a legend in Pennsylvania. I'll always remember sitting there, talking to him about my opportunity to go to Penn State. That meant a lot to me.

The signing date was coming up in February of my senior year. When I was narrowing down my choices, I had decided that I was probably going to attend a different school.

I called an assistant coach at Penn State to let him know I was probably going to go to a different school. I think that surprised him. He asked me, "Hey, did you sign with anybody?" I said, "Well, no, the signing date is a couple weeks away. No, I haven't done that yet." He said, "Well, hold on a second." He got Coach Paterno on the phone. I was trying to avoid talking to Coach Paterno. I just wanted to talk to the assistant. Coach Paterno got on the phone line and said, "Hey, Mike, why don't you ask your mom and dad if it's okay if I come over to your house tomorrow night. Let me come over and have dinner with you and discuss your decision."

Obviously, who's going to say no to Coach Paterno coming over to your house? My parents were thrilled and excited as heck. The next day Coach Paterno was at the house and had dinner with us. We talked. The conversation was not a whole lot about me. He found common ground with my parents on many levels. Then, Coach Paterno asked for a couple minutes alone with me. We talked about my decision on not going to Penn State. I changed my mind that night. Coach Paterno said that he couldn't guarantee that I ever play a down of football at Penn State, but he guaranteed that I'd have the best experience of my life at Penn State. He said I would come out of Penn State with a business degree, which was what I was working for.

He guaranteed that if I had the talent to play, that they'd bring it out in me, and bring out the best in me. If I was afraid of that challenge, then maybe he shouldn't be sitting here, offering me a scholarship. It was a very motivating and honest talk. When he left, I really gave some thought to what he said. I realized what he said to me was exactly what I wanted. What was most important to me was an education from a good school. I also wanted to be challenged to be the best I could be. I really bought into the fact that if anyone could do that, they could. They could bring that out in me, just like he said. A couple days later, I called the coach and changed my mind, and said I wanted to go to Penn State.

You know what your parents want for you. Mine always guided me. They always let me make my own decisions. That was my biggest decision of my life, to that point, for sure. I think my parents wanted to guide me, but not direct me. I've always appreciated that. I knew in the back of my mind what they probably wanted. But still, the decision was mine. When I said I was thinking of not going to Penn State, they were all behind what I was thinking, what my thoughts were.

Joe Paterno

The best example I'll give of what Coach Paterno was like was the fact that he came to my house, had dinner with my parents, and said the things he said to me in a very positive, but challenging way. That told me everything I was in for. That's how he was when I got to Penn State too, honest and disciplined.

I loved the discipline and the way he ran the program. What he said, he did. He taught you a lot of life's lessons. He always related life to football. The first conversation he had with the team, there were about 100 players there. He made it very clear that the next four years were going to be the last four years of football for a high percentage of us. He said, "The next four years are going to be the best years of your life." He also said, "Your education is your priority. You need to leave with that education no matter what happens."

He instilled that from day one, and not just that first day, but weekly. He always talked about life and life's lessons. I think it was very interesting how he found a way, every week, win or lose, to teach us something. I thought that was very unique. I always thought he was a great speaker within the moment. When you left there, I think you appreciated it more. What he meant to the program, what he meant to us, and what he taught me.

I can meet a Penn State guy anywhere, who played for Coach Paterno in any decade, and we have similar stories and similar feelings. That's a nice bond. It was a nice fraternity to be a part of.

Position Played At Penn State
Coach Paterno was honest with me regarding what position I would play. That day, in my house, he said, "I'm not quite sure if you'll ever play. I'm not sure what position you're even going to play." When I got to Penn State, I thought I was going to be a defensive player. Coach Paterno had me on the offensive side from day one. I moved from tight end after a one-day trial, to defensive line, to offensive line. I move from offensive tackle, to guard, and to center. He moved me around. He did the same thing with a lot of players. He had a knack for finding the right fit for you. It seemed like I never really got what I wanted, but I got what I was supposed to get. I thought I knew what I wanted, but I really didn't.

Coach Paterno let the process happen by moving me from position to position. By the beginning of my sophomore year, I found my home on the offensive line, which I developed into. If you told me I was going to be an offensive lineman coming out of high school, I never would have believed it. I think a lot of guys have similar stories. I think he wanted what was best for you. Coach Paterno and his staff were very well trained to do that. I'm sure most college coaches are, but Coach Paterno had a knack. He wasn't going to tell you something that you wanted to hear. He was going to tell you what he felt was the truth.

Penn State's Biggest Rival
Pittsburgh was Penn State's biggest rival. It was awesome. It was always a Thanksgiving Day game. Obviously, I've heard all the stories. For instance, Tony Dorsett and the tradition they had through the '70s. The time in the early '80s when we were there that was the game you waited for. Win the state battle, east versus west. I thought that was the game. Without a doubt, that was the big game. Would it be at our place on Thanksgiving Day, or at their place? I was just happy that they started the rivalry up again, because a lot of people had forgot how strong that was, and what a big game that was.

Option Of Playing One More Season At Penn State
I had the option of playing one more year at Penn State. I came out a year early. I knew what a good team we had. My freshman year I was mainly on special teams and on the practice squad, so I didn't see the field as an offensive player until my sophomore year. I was a starter at guard my whole

sophomore year. Then my junior year I injured my knee in spring training. I had to miss the year and got redshirted.

I came back the next year and started the whole year. I was back to feeling good again. As a young man, I'd never been hurt before like that. The injury spooked me a little bit. The fact was that I was able to graduate in four years and I was able to get healthy. Just about every one of us in my recruiting class was graduating. I just thought the timing was right for me to enter the draft. I had graduated. I had played and had a chance to contribute every year. The timing seemed right.

I think if I were to look back and say, "What if," because who knows what would have happened if I had stayed or didn't stay. I was happy for Penn State when they won the National Championship the next year because, obviously, those guys were all good friends of mine.

Todd Blackledge and Curt Warner did a great job. I was teammates with all those guys. I can't tell you how happy I was for them. My senior year, we were number one for X amount of weeks, and didn't quite get it done that year. I was happy that they were able to do it the next year. I felt like even though I wasn't there, I was a part of it. Any time Penn State has success, I feel like I'm a part of it, one way or another. It was time for me to move on and enter the draft. I was happy for them. I'm not really one who looks back and gets all caught up in that.

NFL Draft
When I heard that talk from Coach Paterno, it didn't mean I didn't have dreams of someday playing in the NFL. I had thought the same thing Coach Paterno said, and I was going to enjoy my four years at Penn State. I wanted to get the best out of my four years. That's what I bought into, when Coach Paterno was in my house. I was going to hold him to that. I wanted the degree in business.

I wanted to play for Penn State, and that's what I was focused on. I really didn't think about the NFL. I saw my teammates getting drafted and I started thinking, "If this guy can get drafted in the NFL, then heck, I have a shot at this thing." I start realizing that if I continued to develop, continued to play, and continued to work hard; I'd have a chance to play on the next level.

I was developing into an offensive lineman. I had a long way to go between gaining weight, gaining strength, and learning the position. A lot was happening in a short period of time for me. Then, I realized ... I did have an opportunity to play in the NFL. Where I'd go and where

I'd get drafted was not something I had any idea of when I became draft eligible. The draft was on a Tuesday back then. It was 12 rounds, six rounds on Tuesday and six rounds on Wednesday. It started at 7:30 in the morning. It's a lot different than it is now. I think it just started being on TV broadcast live on ESPN around 1980. It was exciting.

I wasn't sure what was going to happen. I played in an All-Star game, which helped me quite a bit in moving up in the draft. That's why I feel those All-Star games are valuable. I played in the Olympia Gold Bowl. I remember Marcus Allen was in it. I thought that helped me quite a bit, in the combine. You never know how it's going to work out, but I was told I'd be drafted in the first round. The day of the draft I thought this could be a long morning.

I went to my girlfriend's apartment the morning of the draft so we could just be by ourselves. The draft started at 7:30 in the morning. It was so different than now. It's become such a big production. My parents were two and a half hours away from me. My dad and mom were working.

A team went up there to draft and I knew they weren't looking for offensive linemen. I remember when Houston came up, I thought, "They have talked about drafting a quarterback or an offensive lineman." Jim McMahon had already been drafted a couple picks earlier. I thought, "Oh, you never know. They could draft me" As my name was being called the phone was ringing. It was the head coach of the Houston Oilers congratulating me. I was hearing my name said live on TV.

It's like you go off on a tangent. "Did this really happen?" You're in a fog. It's the weirdest feeling, to hear your name called and knowing that you just got picked by an NFL team to move on to the NFL level. For a 21-year-old man, it was really, really exciting. It's hard to find the words to describe it.

Then, to talk on the phone with the head coach and realize, "Man, I'm going to be blocking for Earl Campbell." That was the first thought that came in my mind. I thought, "This is unbelievable." It was really exciting for my family and me.

That was just a great moment for my family. When I spoke to my family they were all screaming and yelling.

It's just a great family moment for someone from Scranton to first go to Penn State, which was a thrill, and then to have an opportunity to play in the NFL. It was a dream come true. There was just a lot of excitement. I'm happy to have had all the people that helped me along the way, including my high school teammates, my high school coach, Coach Paterno, and Dick Anderson, the Penn State line coach. Dick had taught me how to play on the offensive line, which I've always been so grateful for.

He's the best line coach I've ever been around. I learned so much from him. I left Penn State with a degree, and an occupation. They trained me to be a football player and a businessman. I can't thank Penn State enough for what they did for me.

Joining Houston Oilers
When I got to Houston they were in the beginning of rebuilding the team. They had battled the Steelers all through the '70s. The Pittsburgh Steelers were building their dynasty at the same time the Oilers were.

Unfortunately, the Oilers kept coming in second to the Steelers. By the time the Oilers hit the early '80s, they were rebuilding. They decided to do it through the offensive line. It was exciting to be part of that. Back then there was no free agency. You knew you were probably going to be on the same team for your entire career unless they decided to trade you. Bruce Matthews and Dean Steinkuhler were drafted by the Oilers and were part of the rebuilding process.

I came into the league and there was a strike, so I only played in nine games. The second year was my first full year. We were two and 14. That's what rebuilding brought.

Warren Moon was a free agent out of Canada. When we got him in 1984 he was the biggest piece of the puzzle. Before he came we were building the offensive line.

Obviously, the quarterback is always the most important piece of the puzzle. The Oilers were building through the offensive line and to be able to protect someone like Warren, I think that's what made it come together.

Bruce, Dean, and I learned so much during those years, when we weren't winning. We were playing and growing as players. We knew we were going to be together for a long time. We were hopeful that we were developing something so that we'd be able to win games for a lot of years. It's hard to play, in seasons like that. I think because we were so young and so excited about what we were doing, that made us better players. It's fun to watch them continue to build the team year in, year out, and through draft. That was the main way of building it. There were trades here and there. It was fun to be part of something from the ground level, and watch us build it up to a playoff team for seven years in a row.

It's weird, when you go from college to the pros and you're playing with players you watched on TV, who are years older than you. In high school and in college, you don't have that difference in age.

When you go to the NFL, the age difference is unique. All of a sudden, you're teammates with guys you've watched play that are household names. All of a sudden, you are lining up and blocking for them or blocking with them. That's cool. I think that helped us overcome not winning. Obviously, the goal is to win. We knew we were building something, so patience had to be there. I think as they put the pieces of the puzzle together, like they did, it was exciting to know we were part of that, so we appreciated it much more when we started winning.

Earl Campbell

It was exciting to join the Houston Oilers knowing what kind of team I was going to be part of. For offensive linemen, you just had to get the hell out of Earl Campbell's way because he'd run you over like he did the defensive players. He was a downhill north and south runner. He was faster than people thought. To be a lineman in that type of offense was pretty much a dream come true.

He was a great guy. He took guys under his wing and made them feel comfortable. He was so laid back and full of life. He was a big country guy who would sing Willie Nelson songs on the airplane over the intercom. He was very unique. Me being in Houston, Texas, a guy from Pennsylvania, and being a part of that and knowing even though we weren't winning yet, we were building something special.

Elvin Bethea

One of my first memories with the Houston Oilers was of Elvin Bethea. Elvin was in his 16th year in the NFL when I was in my first year. I'm thinking, "Man, look at this old guy." I'm pass blocking and he's playing defensive end. I had a chance to go against him one-on-one. I figured I was this big rookie who was going to jump all over him. I found out real quickly why he had been around for 16 years. His quickness allowed him to arm-over me so fast as I was trying to kill him.

Veterans On Houston Oilers My Rookie Year

When I came into the league, I saw the way Dave Casper played the game and his work ethic. To experience that as a young player and to see those types of guys early in my career really made a difference in me. I saw how these great players prepared. They didn't take it for granted. That's why they were special. Every year was a new challenge in the NFL.

Archie Manning was our quarterback. So I'm around Archie Manning, who I watched for years playing for the New Orleans Saints. I'm sitting there looking through the Oilers program and seeing all these guys listed. I thought "You're part of this team now. They're expecting you to help them win."

Warren Moon

Warren went to Canada and played in the Canadian Football League because he wanted to play quarterback.

At that time, things were a little bit different in the NFL. NFL teams weren't buying into the fact that quarterback was his best position.

Warren stuck to his guns, what he believed in, and what he felt he was capable of being. Obviously, he proved it. He had a great career in Canada, which allowed him to be one of the first true free agents in the NFL. When left the CFL he was being courted by a lot of teams. We were lucky to get him in Houston.

When he first came in, I saw his size, strength, commitment to the game, and how hard he worked. I knew we had something special.

Bruce Matthews, Dean Steinkuhler, Harvey Salem, and I had been together for a while playing on the offensive line. I remember how excited we were in thinking, "This guy has a chance to be really special. If he's special, he'll make us and finally turn us into a winning football team." There was a lot of excitement in Houston the day the Oilers got Warren and it proved out.

Run and Shoot Offense
Warren Moon adapted to and ran the Run and Shoot offense. Many people don't realize he was doing what Peyton Manning did years later. Warren was calling all the plays and running the system.

Warren and Coach Kevin Gilbride worked really well together. Watching the Run and Shoot grow in the late '80s and early '90s was special.

It took a while to adjust to the Run and Shoot. It was totally different. It was really out of the offensive linemen's comfort zone. The hardest part was figuring out where the quarterback was throwing the ball from. We were so used to the quarterback always being seven yards deep right behind the center.

All of a sudden, we went to an offense where Warren was going to be in a lot of different spots.

Sometimes, he was going to be in the conventional seven-yard drop spot. Then other times, he might be a little bit over the left guard, or a little bit over the right guard, or rolling out. It made the defense have to work a little bit. The defense had trouble designing blitzes and line stunts to attack the quarterback. There were some positives to it, but the fact was you had to realize where Warren was.

The Run and Shoot took a while to figure out. You think you're blocking your guy and the next thing you know, your guy is reaching over and grabbing the quarterback. I would be thinking that the quarterback was in a different location. It took time for the offensive linemen to get used to that and also knowing that we were going to throw the ball quite a bit.

Defensive linemen and fans, want offenses to throw the ball. Defensive linemen want the opportunity to rush the passer. It was a whole different mindset for the offensive linemen.

We still had 1,000-yard rushers in Mike Rozier and Allen Pinkett. We still had Alonzo Highsmith running the football. We had some good years. Obviously, the pass set up the run, rather than the run set up the pass.

It put a lot of pressure on Warren. Warren really had to be on his game week in and week out, because so much of what we were doing was on him. The other thing was it was hard to prepare for games for the offense. We went to the Run and Shoot first then Detroit went to the same system. There was very little film on teams defending the Run and Shoot. So when you were going to play against a team, you had no idea how they were going to play you. If we were going to play the Steelers, Browns, or the Bengals, the teams in our division at the time, we had no idea how they were going to play against our offense. We couldn't watch film of teams playing the Run and Shoot because nobody was using it.

It was hard. You were adjusting during the game, after you saw how the defense was going to play against your team, which was using four wide receivers. This offense was new to the league and not too many teams were doing it at the level we were. We had an idea of what teams were going to do, but until we played a lot of teams more than one time, we really didn't know what to expect from them.

That added another element of uncomfortableness for offensive players, especially offensive linemen. Routes are routes, but for offensive linemen, what we had to do and deal with, there was a lot more to it. It grew us as players. I think it helped Bruce Matthews and me. It may have helped our careers. It helped us learn how to adapt to things, learn how to communicate, and to change our technique. It was a learning process, but I think it helped us become better players.

Toughest Defensive Lineman
When I came into the league, the toughest defensive lineman was probably Randy White. We had a big game with the Dallas Cowboys every year. Back then the preseason was more of a big deal than it is now. The fourth preseason game was like the first game of the season. We had a big showdown with Dallas every year. It was a nationally televised game. John Madden was broadcasting it. Randy White was on the back end of his career, but still one of the best in the league. He was another example of a guy I watched win Super Bowls, and play well with Ed "Too Tall" Jones, and that whole group of guys they had. Playing against a guy like Randy White, as physical, quick, and strong as he was, is something I had never really experienced in college.

One of my first starts in the NFL was during a preseason game my rookie year against the Cowboys. After going against Randy I thought, "Whoa, this is the level of play that I'm going to be dealing with every Sunday." That was my first taste of greatness of going against someone like him. He's the guy that stood out for me because when you're young, and playing against a guy that ends up being a Hall of Famer, is something you always remember.

Bruce Matthews
I always tell Bruce Matthews if it weren't for me, he wouldn't have made the Pro Football Hall Of Fame. His last seven years in the NFL I got a chance to coach him, so I always try to take credit for him.

Obviously, I had nothing to do with his greatness. He played 19 years in the NFL. I saw every play he ever played, which is hard for anyone else to say.

What a relationship. He introduced me into the Pro Football Hall Of Fame, and I introduced him into the Pro Football Hall Of Fame. We were each other's presenters.

My daughters are like daughters to him. With his kids, I feel like I'm the same thing to them—part of the family. We have a very unique relationship. That's rare. We were blessed to be good friends and good teammates for a long time.

Coaching him was interesting. I think it made me a better coach, coaching someone like him. You learn to coach the good ones, the special guys, the regular guys, and all the other different types of players you deal with.

I thought Bruce handled it very professionally. It's not easy to coach guys who were once your teammates. It doesn't happen very often, but it does happen. It was a great time in my life having him in it, and then coaching with him for a while was unique, too. We've had a great NFL relationship. We're obviously best friends. He's been very helpful to me, not only during my playing career, but also during my coaching career. It was great.

We'd be in a meeting, and I'd say, "I'm trying to coach up this great technique." Usually, I'd go overboard with trying to teach it. I'd look at him, and he'd say, "Man, you can't do that." He'd bring me back to reality that something I was trying to teach was a little more difficult than I thought it was. He'd give me that look like, "No, man, that's not happening." He kept me grounded. He didn't let me get too carried away with my coaching, especially as I was learning the trade. He helped me adjust as a coach, too. He gave me great feedback. He was very helpful to me getting started as a coach. I kept adjusting my teaching style in what I said, didn't say, or maybe my routine, by a lot of the input he gave me. It was a big advantage to me being able to coach him.

"The Comeback" Houston Oilers vs. Buffalo Bills In 1993 Playoffs
At halftime we thought we had the 1993 playoff game against the Buffalo Bills won. I'm not going to lie. We played about as good a first half as a team could play, on the road, against the Bills. The Bills had a great defense with Bruce Smith and Darryl Talley. They had a who's who on defense. We went up there and scored 28 points in the first half. The first four times we had the ball on offense, we scored touchdowns. I try to block out some of the bad memories from that game. What I remember was we were going up and down the field. Everything we did, worked. Warren couldn't have thrown the ball any better. We were blocking and we ran the ball when we wanted to. It was 28-3 at halftime. At halftime, we thought, "We're playing at the level we're supposed to play at." The run and shoot was clicking as good as it could be clicking.

We knew that we had to play a whole second half, but obviously we felt very strong about our position. Then, the second half happened and unfortunately it was the total opposite for us from onside kicks to balls bouncing the wrong way.

The Bills drove down and scored, then they kicked an onside kick and got the ball and scored again. Warren threw one ball, it got tipped, and it turned into an interception. The Bills scored 14 points before we got the ball at one point. The Bills scored 28 points in the third quarter. Then we knew it was going to be a game. When that happened, game on. At the end of the fourth quarter we were tied.

There still was overtime, and I thought we'd overcome everything. We thought we were still going to win the football game, and we didn't.

The worst part was not going through it one time, but you have to live it the rest of your life. Every time the playoffs are about to start, networks are still playing that game over again on TV. It's one of those things where it's a memory I really don't want to have to relive. I'm thinking, "Wasn't that long enough ago? Why do they keep playing that game?" Unfortunately, it seems like some people still say, "Oh yeah, I saw you in the game."

It's not a great memory but credit goes to the Bills. They were a great football team. They went to four Super Bowls in a row at that time. Jim Kelly wasn't even playing in that game so we had no excuse. It wasn't like we could say, "Oh, Jim, man, Jim." Frank Wright led the charge. He did a great job, as the Bills quarterback that day. As good as we were in the first half was as bad as the Bills were. The first half was amazing. In the second half we flipped roles. The Bills somehow made enough plays to beat us.

That's why I was so happy when I went into coaching with the Tennessee Titans and the "Music City Miracle" was against the Bills and we won. So that was my settling grace, that day. We were the Titans at the time, which obviously were the former Oilers. My payback as a player and a coach was that I returned the favor in a very memorable way.

Pro Football Hall Of Fame Induction

I'll remember the day I found out I was selected for the Pro Football Hall Of Fame forever. I was at home in Nashville, Tennessee. I was a coach for the Tennessee Titans. I knew I was one of the 15 finalists.

I had talked to John McClain who was the reporter that represented me before the voters. Every finalist has a representative from their NFL city that is reminding voters of the player's achievements. We had talked and he said, "You've got a shot." That was about it.

He said, "We'll probably be making the announcement by 11:00 a.m. on Saturday. I'll call you as soon as I know something, either way." My daughter was playing basketball in the YMCA League on that Saturday. I thought the basketball game would keep me busy, and keep the Hall Of Fame decision off my mind. I decided I'm not going to make a big production out of this. Both of my daughters were young at the time, so I didn't want to get everyone all caught up in it. I just played it low key.

We were getting ready to go to the basketball game, and I saw the clock and thought, "Man, I didn't hear anything." I thought that meant I didn't make it. I wasn't giving much thought to it, but I decided to turn the on TV and see who made it. I turned the on TV and I found ESPN. The sportscaster said, "They've been delayed. The team hasn't been announced yet. They'll be announcing the decision in the next few minutes."

I hadn't heard from John yet, so I figured, "Well, I'm going to wait and see who made it." I sat down. My daughters were getting ready for the game. I was in the room by myself. The director of the Hall Of Fame came out and started announcing the names. The director said, "This is in random order." The third or fourth name was mine. Just to hear it—wow. I couldn't believe I heard it. At the same time, just like when I got drafted by the Oilers, the phone was ringing. It was John, screaming into the phone about how happy he was about me getting into the Hall Of Fame. My family came in the room. My wife was jumping around. It was a great family moment. Almost like when I came into the league and got drafted. What do you say about something like that? It was an unbelievable experience. Then the phone rang off the hook for the next 24 hours.

What I like about the induction it's a celebration. All of the people that were a part of your career and have been a part of your experience have an opportunity to go to Canton to be a part of the celebration with you. What a great way to do it. That's why that weekend is so special; it's not just about you. It's about everybody, your immediate family, your football family, your high school, and your college family.

Photograph copyright Associated Press

Chapter 10

Morten Anderson

College:
Michigan State

Career History:
New Orleans Saints (1982–1994)
Atlanta Falcons (1995–2000)
New York Giants (2001)
Kansas City Chiefs (2002–2003)
Minnesota Vikings (2004)
Atlanta Falcons (2006–2007)

2017 Inductee Pro Football Hall Of Fame

College Choice
Purdue University, Albion College, Delaware, and some smaller schools recruited me. In 1977, I was an exchange student from Copenhagen Denmark. We had a really good team that year. We had a lot of good players who were recruited by colleges and I happened to be one of them. A couple months into the season I was recruited by Michigan State. It happened fairly quickly.

A guy named Bob Baker, the offensive coordinator at Michigan State, came down to recruit me. He had been in the CFL for a many years. Hans Nielsen, another Danish kicker who was at Michigan State, also came down to recruit me. He convinced me that if he could do it I could probably do it, too. That was a big factor in me ending up as a Spartan.

I just picked up kicking when I came to the United States. I barely spoke the language when I came to the United States. It was a little bit of a culture shock, but I actually picked it up pretty fast. I landed in the United States on my 17th birthday, and two days later I was kicking field goals for the high school team. I all happened very fast.

Biggest Rivalry In College
Our biggest rival was Michigan, for sure. We beat them my freshman year 24-15.

I had a lot of respect for Bo Schembechler and his teams. Playing in the Big House in Ann Arbor was pretty cool, obviously. Spartan Stadium was equally as fun, but being in front of 105,000 people against Michigan was pretty mind-blowing.

We won the Big Ten my very first year at Michigan State. We had great players in Eddie Smith, Kirk Gibson, and Mark Brammer along with other really good players. When we beat Michigan my freshman year I thought, "Oh, let's do that every year." But, that was the only time in four years we beat them.

We would have played in the Rose Bowl my freshman year, but we were on probation because of the previous head coach, Denny Stolz. Since we were on probation, we were banned from postseason play. I never played in a bowl game.

Being on probation was a bad deal, but it was really none of our doing. It happened because of the previous administration. I really don't know what the reason was for us going on probation because it happened before I got there. We inherited that problem.

Kirk Gibson

Kirk Gibson was great. He was just a great athlete. He led by example and was a true leader on the field. He was an All-American in baseball and in football. He probably would have been drafted in the first round of the NFL Draft if he had decided to play wide receiver in the NFL.

63-Yard Field Goal Against Ohio State

The 63-yard field goal that I made against Ohio State is the longest I've ever kicked in a game. Unfortunately, it wasn't big in the context of the outcome of the game because we got our ass kicked by Ohio State. The kick was before halftime. It was a big moment in my history and a big moment in Spartan history, but unfortunately, it didn't help us win the game.

The kick was at Ohio State in the Horseshoe. I had a little bit of wind behind me, but it was a big kick. I hit it well.

NFL Draft

I had no idea the Saints were going to draft me. I had no communication with them at all. It was a big surprise to me that they took me in the fourth round.

I suppose there were big expectations from New Orleans for me. New Orleans first round draft choice a couple years earlier had been Russell Erxleben, a punter and placekicker from the University of Texas. He had not worked out very well for New Orleans.

Obviously they hoped picking me would work out better. Thank God it did. I was just trying to make the football team. I didn't really think about any of the expectations on me, or the history of New Orleans kickers, or the ramifications. I was just trying to make kicks and get onto the football team.

1982 NFL Players Strike

I was recovering from an injury during the NFL Players Strike. I got hurt on the very first play of my NFL career, the opening kickoff of the season. I was out for eight weeks. The strike actually worked in my favor. It gave me a chance to rehab and get healthy again so when the strike was over, I could continue playing. If the strike hadn't come then I would have missed a ton of games.

Bum Phillips

I loved Bum Phillips. He was like a dad to everybody. Everything was a family atmosphere with the New Orleans Saints. We played for each other. We won some games. We would have liked to have won a few more and gotten into the playoffs with Bum as our head coach, but it didn't happen. We had a lot of big moments together. I just loved the man. He was just a great mentor and a great father figure to me.

Jim Mora

Jim Mora was the polar opposite of Bum Phillips. He was completely different than Bum. In defense of Jim and his policy, Bum's way hadn't worked in that we hadn't gone to the next level. We had won with Bum but we really hadn't won consistently and hadn't gone to the playoffs. So that was the mandate that Jim Mora had been given by Jim Finks and Tom Benson, the new owner.

There were a lot of changes made in the front office of the Saints organization and Mora was obviously given the responsibility of turning the team around. He felt the way he had to do it was with more discipline and more structure. With that in mind he assembled the type of team that he wanted and we won a lot of games with Mora.

New Orleans Saints Team With Jim Mora As Head Coach
We had a great defense. Our defensive line consisted of Jim Wilks and Frank Warren. Both guys were great players along with our linebackers.

We kicked a lot of field goals. We had ball control in that we didn't turn the ball over. We ran the ball effectively. Bobby Hebert was a great quarterback for us. Our offense possessed the ball, moved the chains, and scored in the red zone. A lot of our scores would be 15- 12 or we would win by a lot of field goals. That's really what we did.

Being A Kicker In the NFL
I felt like I was an integral part of the game. I was busy and that kept me in the game. I loved that. I just felt like, "Hey, they're using me. They feel like I can be an offensive weapon, and let me embrace it." That's what I tried to do.

I always felt like I was part of the teams that I played for. I never felt like I was a separate entity or anything. I know my skill was unique and specific, but I always felt like I was a part of the team. I respected my teammates and they had respect for me.

60-Yard Field Goal Against Chicago Bears
On the 60-yard field goal against the Chicago Bears, that ball was hit really well. That could have been good from 70 yards. In retrospect, it would have been nice breaking the record.

Kicking In A Dome
I never gave that much credence to whether kicking in a dome helped me make the Pro Football Hall Of Fame. My numbers were just as good outside in the elements as they were inside. I feel like I could be, and I was effective. I had big years kicking outside for Kansas City and New York. For me, that was the hand I was dealt. I played for two teams for twenty-one years (the Falcons and the Saints) that happened to play inside. Had they played outside I would have been fine.

Biggest Kick In NFL
I hate to pick one kick out as the biggest, but certainly the one in overtime in the NFC Championship Game against the Minnesota Vikings was big because it sent us to the Super Bowl. A lot of good things happened before that kick as well. That was a big kick, a big moment, but all kicks have the same value so I'd like to think they're all important in their own way. That one was the last play of the game in overtime to go to the Super Bowl, so I would probably say that had the biggest impact.

It felt great to get to the Super Bowl, but it felt equally as bad not winning the game. I was grateful that I did make the Super Bowl, but very disappointed we didn't win the game.

Again, it is one of those things. It wasn't meant to be for me.

Key To Successfully Kicking For 25 Seasons In NFL
The key to my success was just hard work; persistence, will, stubbornness, and having great people around me that did their job really well at a high level. Also, having great communication between all of us is what we needed to play at a high level. I think that's probably the key for me.

Evolution Of Kicking Style As Grew Older
I managed my behavior better as I grew older. I kicked less, but I had more quality kicks. I really dialed in and honed in on my skill. I knew mentally exactly what I needed to do, and I understood my workbench where that ball is put down. I really understood my job and defined my job, and I was able to execute what I needed to do. I think in the beginning of my career I was probably winging it more. I think as I matured I probably became a little more methodical, a little more thought out, if you will.

Long Snappers & Holders
Whoever my long snapper was, I was going to make sure that I communicated to him what I needed from him, which was his very best. I didn't accept it if a holder thought he could just put the ball down randomly. That was unacceptable. I also didn't accept it if a long snapper thought he could just snap it randomly. I demanded from those guys, at those two positions, that they knew exactly what they were doing. And, I demanded that they could do it consistently again and again, because that's what was expected out of me. I felt like the three of us worked like fingers in a glove. It was very important that we were on the same page, that they told me what they needed, and I told them what I needed from them. Then there was a trust where we didn't overthink it. When that was clearly laid out, we worked on the skill and we trusted it when we played.

My Best Holder & Long Snapper
Dan Stryzinski was my best holder. He had the best hands. He understood exactly what to do with different snaps if they came in weird. Kendall Gammon was my best long snapper by far in Kansas City. He was an artist. He knew exactly what to do with the ball and he put it in the right place. I was very lucky to have those two guys in Kansas City for two years.

Becoming All-Time Leading Scorer In NFL History
When I became the all-time leading scorer it was special. It felt like a culmination of a long journey. It wasn't a "me" award; it was more of a "we" award again because so many people had helped me along the way. It was very gratifying when the game was stopped briefly and I was able to hand the jersey to my oldest son and get the game ball. It was certainly a nice moment.

Not Playing During the 2005 Season
After the 2004 season I was out for 20 months. During that time I practiced in a public park. I felt very strongly that I would be back. I didn't know it was going to take 20 months until I got a phone call and had an opportunity to come back, but that's what happened.

I thank God I was ready because it could have gone terribly wrong had I not been prepared. In 2006 when the call came to try out and win the job, I was ready to go and got plugged in.

I had a good year and was able to break the scoring record. I played again in 2007. So it was just a matter of having the stubbornness and the will to continue even though most people might have said, "You're probably done."

Not Having the Opportunity To Break George Blanda's Record For Being Oldest Player In NFL History

I tried to come back in 2008, but there were no takers. When I realized that it was probably going to be over, I retired on the day after I would have been the oldest player in NFL history had I played. It was more of a nod towards George Blanda and what he accomplished.

I don't know why no teams signed me in 2008. That's a question you would have to ask all of the different player personnel guys working in 2008. At that time I wasn't kicking off anymore, and I think my range had diminished. I was pretty good from 50 yards in, but everybody goes younger and cheaper. I'm sure that's what happened.

Pro Football Hall Of Fame Selection

When I found out I was selected for the Pro Football Hall Of Fame I experienced a lot of emotions. Relief was one of them. I no longer had to justify, "I did this, this, and this." Now it was an even playing field and I became a part of an exclusive brotherhood. I thought that was unique. It was a unique feeling. The history of excellence among those 310 players who are in the Pro Football Hall Of Fame is incredible. I have tremendous pride and gratitude towards everyone who helped me along the way.

Photograph copyright Associated Press

Chapter 11

Bruce Matthews

> College:
> USC
>
> Career History:
> Houston/Tenessee Oilers/Titans (1983-2001)
>
> As Coach:
> Houston Texans (2009–2010) (offensive assistant)
> Tennessee Titans (2011–2013) (offensive line)
>
> 2007 Inductee Pro Football Hall Of Fame

College Choice
The primary reason I went to USC was that my brother Clay went there and had a great experience. I became a huge fan of USC.

I was getting recruited heavily. My intention was that if USC offered me a scholarship, that's where I wanted to go. They were the defending national champions in football. USC was a half-hour from where I grew up. I went to all of Clay's home games and became a huge USC fan.

Head Coach John Robinson
To this day, I have a great deal of respect for Coach John Robinson and the type of head coach that he was. As an 18-year-old kid going to USC, Coach Robinson really made a big impact on my life. Not to say that other coaches are different, but I think at that time of my life, Coach Robinson just emphasized no individual is bigger than the team.

We had some huge individuals. We had Charles White, Marcus Allen, Ronnie Lott, and Anthony Munoz. As a young player it was apparent to me that all of those guys had completely bought into the way Coach Robinson did business. I just had great respect for him, and to this day I still have great respect for him.

USC Offensive Line
My freshman year, we had six future NFL first round draft picks just on the offensive line. They were Anthony Munoz, Brad Budde, Keith Van Horne, Roy Foster, Don Mosebar, and me. All those guys taught me about what it really meant to practice hard and to play hard.

You tend to get a higher opinion of yourself than reality dictates. Being around those guys and seeing their professionalism at such a young age really had a huge impact on my career.

USC Talent
Going into USC, I remember thinking, "Man, these guys are pretty good." We were good not only on the offensive line, but at every position group.

My first year at USC we were blowing teams out and I was playing the better part of the second half in most of the games. Unfortunately, we tied Stanford my freshman year. We were up 21-0 against Stanford and they came back to tie the game. I thought at some point we'd definitely win a championship, but it didn't work out that way.

John Elway played against us in the Stanford game, but it was Turk Schonert who did the lion's share of the quarterbacking. As I recall, Elway didn't have that great of a game. It was one of many comebacks I've been involved in. Fortunately, or unfortunately, it ended up in a tie.

I am hard pressed to think of anybody who would have beaten us my freshman year. I think Alabama won the National Championship that year. I'm biased of course, but I think we'd have beat up on Alabama if we played them that year. In fact, the year before, USC went down to Birmingham to play and crushed Alabama.

NFL Draft
The Houston Oilers had expressed interest in me prior to the draft. Bill Parcells was the new Giants Head Coach in 1983. At the Tampa combine that year, Bill came up to me and introduced himself. Bill said if I was available at number ten, the Giants were drafting me. It was a thrill. I have always been a Bill Parcells fan as a result of this. The Oilers made a couple deals that year, and moved back to pick nine and took me. I wasn't surprised they took me, but I wasn't banking on it either.

Rookie Year With Houston Oilers
As a rookie, everything was so new and cool. I was walking around on cloud nine. Like man, they actually pay me to play football. I don't know that any coach would have had a different impact on my first year because it was just such a thrill to be there.

Earl Campbell
One of the highlights of my career was playing with Earl Campbell. I played a year-and-a- half with him. He rushed for like 1,300 or 1,400 yards my rookie year. I missed a bunch of time my rookie year due to injury. As a kid who grew up in complete awe of the NFL experience, to get to know Earl a little bit, to see he was a legit guy, experience his whole country boy persona, and see he was genuine, was the best. It really was an honor to play with him. It's something I'm really proud of.

Jerry Glanville As Houston Oilers Head Coach
There were pluses and minuses with Jerry Glanville as Houston Oilers Head Coach, obviously. I think the biggest plus was Jerry did a great job of taking a team that had talent and making us believe. We played hard under Jerry.

An opposing team is going to give you their best shot. You don't ever want to empower the enemy. You don't want to give the opponent anything that may be bulletin board material, or something along those lines. Jerry inflamed some of our opponents, or most, I should say. But to his credit, he took a team that was a sleeping giant and woke us up. He was a huge part of getting us on that big playoff run in the late '80s thru early '90s.

Building Houston Oilers Offensive Line Thru Using High Draft Choices On Offensive Lineman
There have been teams that have tried to use the model of building a strong offensive line thru using high draft picks on offensive lineman. Some of those high number ones didn't hit for teams. It's been cool to see the current Dallas Cowboys basically use that model. It's paid huge dividends for the Cowboys with Zack Martin, Travis Frederick, and Tyron Smith.

It reminds me of our Oilers team because our offensive line played a solid nine or ten years together. It's a luxury that you don't appreciate until you don't have it. In a lot of ways, it's taken for granted when you have quality offensive line play because so much of the credit goes to the quarterback, receivers, and running back, and rightfully so. Then all of the sudden, when you have those holes in the offensive line, the good old days are definitely missed.

Run and Shoot/Red Gun Offense
June Jones was kind of the architect of the Run and Shoot Offense. I think the Run and Shoot was an offshoot of the talent that we had.

Warren Moon was such a special talent. We gave him time to throw the ball and had receivers. That being said, we still ran the ball well. The Run and Shoot Offense definitely put more pressure on the offensive line and on the offense in terms of situations where you're trying to run the clock out, or just trying to grind it out, whether it's short yardage or goal line.

During June Jones first years with the team, we ran a conventional offense, two-one-two, multiple tight end sets, and then we would go to the Red Gun. The Red Gun was playing four wide receivers with one running back. Over the years we went more and more exclusively to the Run and Shoot Offense. When Jack Pardee came in we ran the Run and Shoot full time. It definitely did add challenges to us as linemen, but you always looked at it as a challenge and said, "We're going to make this work."

Warren Moon
I think we all struggled early on. Warren Moon came to the Houston Oilers my second year in the NFL. We were a young and talented team and we were emerging. You could see why the Oilers management went out and got Warren. He would make the throws. June Jones came in and really started to utilize Warren's talents.

Warren was a special guy. The thing I think that gets overlooked most about Warren is his durability. He did a great job of preparing himself for the season by being in the best shape he could be, including the mental side of it. He was a pro about it.

Through the years, you see quarterbacks that can stay healthy, whether it's Brett Favre, Tom Brady, or guys like Warren Moon. That is a gift they have. It's the little things that are taken for granted that you don't appreciate until they're gone.

"The Comeback" Houston Oilers vs. Buffalo Bills 1993 Playoff Game
The loss to the Buffalo Bills in the 1993 playoffs was hard. I'll be honest; I couldn't stand it anytime we lost. The part that wasn't as painful as it probably could have been was the fact that it was such a freakish deal. You have teams come back and make plays and maybe get a rally, but you somehow find a way to right the ship and you close the deal. Obviously that wasn't the case against Buffalo, and it was almost like, man, this is bigger than us.

This is one of those once in a lifetime deals. The funny thing was, we had to drive the ball late in the game and kick a field goal to send it into overtime. I thought that the fact that we persevered and found a way to make plays in spite of all the points that they scored and all the momentum being in their favor, I felt like, man, we're going to win this thing.

We won the coin toss in overtime, and Warren Moon threw an interception. Buffalo kicked a field goal and won. That was that.

Super Bowl XXXIV St. Louis Rams vs. Tennessee Titans
The St. Louis Rams completely dominated us in the first two-and-a- half quarters of the game. Then in tightened

fashion, we kind of bludgeon them. Steve McNair made some amazing plays and kept plays alive with his legs. We finally got in position to score, and sent it to overtime. The Rams were done.

I usually don't watch videos of games. Come playoff time, stations always play Super Bowl XXXIV on either the NFL network or other networks. Or, they play the Buffalo playoff game. During those games, there's a part of me that has a certainty within myself that we're going to win this game, even though I know the facts; I know the history.

In my opinion, it was a foregone conclusion that had we gone to overtime, we were going to win, because defensively they were toast. Unfortunately, we were one yard short. It was a great experience to finally get to the Super Bowl. Even the game itself was the culmination of a lot of stuff that the team had gone through, because of our move from Houston. It easily could have gone the other way. It's still frustrating I guess, to sum it up.

Setting Record For Most Games Played By Non Kicker Or Punter With the added perspective of time being out of the game and coaching in the league for five years, I see guys injured or tweaked or whatever, and rightfully so, they're sitting out games. I look back on my career and I felt a high responsibility to be out there every game. I really didn't play in a game where I shouldn't have. There were times I didn't feel 100%. I knew once I got warmed up that I wasn't a detriment to the team; that I was playing at a level that I would be satisfied with how I was playing.

I look back on it and I did all the workouts. I was very diligent in that regard. When I look back, it's a very humbling thing. I think the good Lord just blessed me with a body that could take the pounding. He gave me a tolerance for pain. I don't feel like there ever was a game that I went into where I thought, "Oh my gosh, my leg, or my knee, or my back, or whatever the case might be, I shouldn't be out here."

I felt good when I got out there. Now, the warming up process or getting into it might have taken some effort or some extra special preparation, but I always felt good about it. I look at it as God blessed me, and I'm thankful for that. It's a humbling thing, especially when I got on the coaching side, and saw how many times freak injuries occurred or just weird stuff a guy got hurt on, got tweaked, and had to miss time. I was just blessed. I can't think of how many piles there were, where I got rolled up or the pile fell into my leg, and I was able to get up and walk away.

Father Clay Matthews, Sr.
My dad taught me how to approach a game in terms of attitude and having the right perspective. Early on, he taught our whole family that if you go out there, you don't quit. You go full speed at everything and you're the first guy in line. If the coach asks for a volunteer, raise your hand and make them tell you to stop volunteering or whatever the case may be. That really stuck with me. He instilled in us the mindset to go out and do our best. It really was huge.

Toughest Defensive Lineman
It's hard for me to say who the toughest lineman I ever faced was. I feel bad sometimes singling a guy out. There have been so many great players. When it was game week and we were prepping for them, there was added anxiety having to play them that week. There always was anxiety for me in terms of my opponents and preparing for them. There definitely were some real special ones like Bruce Smith, Howie Long, and John Randle. There are so many good ones. The cool thing about the NFL is that you're tested every week. You may not have heard about a guy, or what college he went to, but in some way (it may be in the run game, it may be in the pass game, it may be backside cutting off whatever the case may be),

he's got some unique skill or talent that if you lower your guard, relax, or get complacent, you're going to be embarrassed.

The thrill of the NFL is knowing you've got to stay on edge the whole game every week, every position, every guy, first and second string. It's been kind of cool to go through that again with my sons, and having those conversations, especially with Jake playing left tackle. There are so many special players that you have to bring it every play.

One of the biggest, if not the most important, traits for an offensive lineman is playing consistent. You can't be one of those guys that has eight great plays and then two busts. You've got to bring it every play. Consistency is more important than those flash plays where you go and put some guy on his back. That's great, but I would rather have you be consistent ten plays than have those eight and two, or nine and one play series.

Trash Talking
Some of the stuff guys said would make me laugh. You're out on the football field trying to keep this edge of almost hatred toward your opponent, because you don't want to give them anything. All of a sudden they're making these chirps out there and it's like, hey, that was pretty clever. The funny thing was, the guys who do the trash talking, most of them make you think, "What are you, an idiot?" It was the quiet ones that you had to worry about. John Randle and Warren Sapp actually had some good humor. It's such an odd place to appreciate humor. You can appreciate it the next day, but while you're out there in the heat of battle, it's something you never really think about.

Pro Football Hall Of Fame Induction
I was a huge fan of the NFL growing up. Although my dad played before I was born, I was very proud of that fact. I never hesitated to share it with buddies at school or something along those lines. I was so proud of my brother Clay when went into the league five years before me. Naturally I was a huge Browns fan because of Clay. I grew up in awe of the league. Playing in the league for 19 seasons, making the Pro Bowl and all that type stuff to me was like, man, I can't believe I'm actually doing this. I think in a lot of ways, in terms of my faith and how I viewed God's relationship to this whole thing, I became so much more humble about it. I realized God blessed me to be able to go out and play this great game. This was nothing that I did on my own. God gave me the body, desire, mindset, and intellect to play the game. The whole process humbled me.

Then, being named to the Hall of Fame was the culmination of all these things. It was like, thank you Lord, for blessing me. I see so much of how this is such a group effort, from my parents and the example that they set, to the opportunity to grow up with a big brother like Clay. I was so blessed. It was a very humbling experience. I was very apprehensive about the Hall of Fame weekend and activities because the spotlight's on you for four full days.

I remember thinking I just can't wait until this is over, because I don't want to be in the spotlight anymore. I'm very appreciative, but this amazing thing happened during that weekend. I got up there and initially started feeling anxious about it. Then I saw how much all my friends and family were enjoying the moment, and it really became a special kind of opportunity to see them enjoying the process and the weekend. All of a sudden, it was no longer about me. I was able to enjoy their responses. It was really cool.

Again, it was just another lesson in humility. It was all about my anxiety and me. I didn't want to be the center of attention. The minute I didn't make it about me, I enjoyed myself.

Photograph copyright Associated Press

Chapter 12

Terrell Davis

College: Long Beach State Georgia Career History: Denver Broncos (1995-2002) 2017 Inductee Pro Football Hall Of Fame

College Choice

I played so many positions in high school. I played five positions; nose guard, linebacker, fullback, kicker, and tight end. I really wasn't a standout athlete in high school. Because I played so many positions, it gave me a great sense of every aspect of the game, from running to tackling to kicking the ball.

My high school, Lincoln High School, was a small school. We only had about 25 players, so we had to play both defense and offense. Prior to that, I had grown up playing running back my entire life.

That's the only position I played from Pop Warner until I got to high school. I couldn't get on the field because Lincoln already had two running backs that were starting. I had to find a way to get onto the field and I did that. I enjoyed playing the game, trying to make a difference, and not getting credit for it. That was fun. Then when it was time to find a college, it kind of counted against me, because I didn't have a position.

My brother was at Long Beach State. Long Beach State came around. They had just gotten George Allen as their head coach. I think my brother had mentioned to them that there was a kid in San Diego they should look at. They didn't know we were brothers, because my brother's last name is Webb. George Allen called because he liked what he saw. He said, "Hey, just come here. We can't promise you anything, but we will promise that if you work hard, we will try hard to take care of you." I guess that meant give me a scholarship. The other schools that were in the picture were Utah State, Pacific, and Cal StateFullerton. No real big schools were recruiting me. Those schools were my only options.

George Allen

George Allen was a defensive minded coach. He spent most of his time on that side of the ball. When I redshirted all I was doing was scout team stuff. That's really where I got back my running back position. I was on the scout team, and Coach Allen wanted the scout team offense to be as good as the starting offense. He thought that was the way you prepare your starting defense. He fell in love with me. He even gave me the nickname, Secretariat. The way he ran special teams, scout team, and meetings, everything was the first taste of a professional team that I had experienced. He had wisdom and knowledge. He was real big on playing together. He had a sign when you walked into our building, which said, "Togetherness

53 men playing together, you can't lose."

I got a chance to work with him very closely because of the fact that he wanted his scout team offense to be extremely good against the defense. I remember times at a Thursday practice when the defense was trying to get off the field, but I'm making them repeat the plays because I'm running so hard. The members of the defense would be getting upset, telling me to slow down and stop running so hard, but George Allen respected that. That's what he taught me, how to practice and play at a certain level all the time. I have a profound respect for George. I learned a lot from him. Although he passed away the year after my redshirt freshman year, I tried to take what I learned from him and use that when I went to Georgia, and then when I went into the pros.

Recruitment After Long Beach State Program Disbanded

There were three schools that were recruiting me after Long Beach disbanded the football program. The first school that had contacted me was Hawaii. UCLA contacted me, but they weren't serious. They had a lot of running backs that they were trying to give scholarships to. They invited me to come down on an unofficial visit, and I did. I was excited about UCLA; I loved UCLA. I thought I was going there.

As a kid growing up in southern California, the big schools were USC and UCLA. I loved UCLA and I loved their colors. I was thinking man, UCLA, that'd be perfect, but they weren't committed. They never offered me a scholarship.

Then I'm sitting there trying to think, should I stay at Long Beach State, should I go to UCLA, or should I go to Hawaii? I didn't really want to go to Hawaii, I just didn't.

When I was thinking about what I should do, I got a call in my room from Bob Pittard from the University of Georgia. He left a message that said, "Hey, give me a call. We'd like to bring you down for a visit." I heard that phone call, and I was shocked. I didn't know much about Georgia at the time, but I knew they had a big program. I did some research. I was telling people about the call, and they were like, "Man, Georgia called you?" Everybody was surprised, even more so than me. They sent me their media guide, so I looked at the players they had in the past, the bowl games they went to, and what conference they were in. It was a no-brainer. I called them and I went there on a visit. I fell in love with the place. I had never seen anything like it. When I was going back to the airport to go home, they pulled me off the shuttle bus and offered me a scholarship. I accepted immediately.

I was a little nervous about going to Georgia because I was a west coast kid. I hadn't really left the west coast and was a little concerned about that. I took a chance and stayed there. It was exciting taking a chance to go to a place not really knowing what to expect. At that time I was 18 or 19 years old. I felt like it was good for my development just go somewhere different. If I didn't like it I, could always go back home. That's kind of how I thought.

Getting Hurt Early In Senior Season In College

I thought there was no way I was going to play in the NFL when I got hurt my senior season in college. I missed a substantial amount of games my senior season and I hadn't had a great college career. Things weren't looking good for me. I remember reflecting on my career while I was sitting in the stands watching the team at one of our home games. I was thinking there's a good chance that I might not ever get a chance to play again for Georgia. Not that I wouldn't come back from my injury, but even if I came back from my injury, there was no guarantee that I was going to play. Hines Ward was our running back at the time and he was playing well. I didn't think I was going to be able to get back on the field once I was healthy.

I thought if I ever get a chance to play again, I've got to play this game differently. It wasn't to make it to the pros. I wanted to finish my college career where I could be proud, where I could look back and say I ended my career on a high note. That was my only goal at that point. I thought the NFL was gone. I didn't think there was any chance I could play in the NFL. I just wanted to try to do it for myself, to just play the game and leave on a high note. It really gave me some motivation. When I got back, I just gave it my all. I didn't care. I just played the game as if I was never going to play the game again. That was kind my mentality for the last four games.

Two of those last games, I played fullback. Hines was the halfback. Before the Auburn game, my coach pulled me into a room and said, "Hey, we've been seeing something different from you, and we like what we see. We're going to put you back as the starting tailback." Auburn was undefeated at the time. I had two more games to play, Auburn and Georgia Tech. Those last two games were probably the two best all around games I had in my college career. I don't know if those two games got me drafted, but I think they got me into the Blue-Gray game. The Blue-Gray game was important because it kept my college career and football career alive. The draft came, and Denver drafted me.

Ray Goff

Ray Goff and I had a difficult relationship. It was not the type of relationship that I would have loved to have with my head coach. For whatever reason, maybe because he was a young coach and I was a young player, we just butted heads. We were like oil and water. We just did not get along.

Some scouts told me things that he had said about me. They said he was attacking my character by saying I wasn't tough. They also said that he was withholding tapes of me. It wasn't stuff that I was making up; these were things I was hearing from scouts. I was upset. At the time, I couldn't understand why a coach would do that. You would think a coach would try to promote you to the pros, so the program looks good and he looks good.

We had a nasty relationship in college. It's been a long time, and Ray and I have spoken a number of times since college. We're actually pretty good friends now. We talk a lot on the phone now. He'll be in Canton for my enshrinement.

We've had a chance to talk, and understand what happened then, and why it happened. I had reached out to him just to let him know that my heart was heavy with what happened, and I didn't feel right carrying that. I had already forgotten about it, really, and then people would bring it up. I'd say, "You know what, I don't feel the same way about Ray. That was years ago. How I felt then and how I feel about him now … I don't feel the same way."

I actually thanked him. I said, "I didn't think about it at the time, but sometimes when somebody's put in your life and they're doing things that in the end make you better, like being hard on you, you may not accept it at the time. You don't like it because you think they're just being hard on you. I believe in God, I believe there's a purpose for everything, and I believe when someone does something, it's for a reason. It's to build character; to make you into the person that you are meant to be. We've gotten past that. College, from that standpoint, was difficult.

NFL Draft

I had no idea the Denver Broncos were going to draft me. I had never heard of the Broncos coming to a pro day for me. They may have come, but they certainly didn't contact me. I didn't hear from an agent or anybody saying they had an interest in me. I don't remember interviewing for the Broncos.

The two teams I thought that showed the most interest in me were the Browns and Cowboys. I had thought maybe one of those teams would draft me. I was hoping the Cowboys drafted me, but they drafted Sherman Williams in the second round. There weren't a lot of pro teams that showed interest.

Starting For Denver Broncos In First Game Of Rookie Season What's even more unbelievable than my starting my first game of my rookie season with the Denver Broncos is that every place I've been, I've had the same route. When I went to Long Beach State I was at the bottom of the depth chart and had to fight my way to the top. I end up starting my redshirt freshman year.

I go to Georgia and I'm sixth or seventh on the depth chart. During training camp I'm behind Garrison Hearst. Then, I'm starting during my junior year.

I've always loved playing running back. I think I was a natural tailback. When I got to Denver, I decided I was going to play this game as if it was the last time I was playing it.

At Georgia, the coach changed the entire offense my junior year. We changed the offense from a more running offense to a more passing one. I was catching the ball out of the backfield more than I was running it. I had to pick up the blitz and I had to catch the ball out of the backfield. It helped me to become a more well-rounded back.

When I got to Denver, their offense suited me well since I could do it all. We played the West Coast Offense, so I had to block, catch, and run. I had to be able to look up and see what coverage the defense was in, their fronts. I thought I had a bit of an advantage because of my college offense.

I was willing to do whatever it took. I did whatever I had to do. When I got my chance to play, it was running down on a kickoff and having to tackle somebody. I felt that I did that and showed I was willing to do anything; they would give me a chance at what I really want to do which was play running back. That was my approach, and it worked.

Timing was everything for me with Denver. I can't say that if I had gone to a team that had an established coach, staff, and running back, that I would have been given a shot at starting at running back. For Mike Shanahan to come in and have this open competition during his first year as Broncos head coach, and not just peg one guy as his starter helped. He was looking to build the team, and didn't have a lot of guys at that time that were already set in positions. He had a few guys, but not enough. He obviously gave me a chance to work my way up. I just liked his approach. He didn't care whether you were a free agent, a low round draft pick, or a first round draft pick. They were going to play the best person. That's all anybody can ask for. That's why I respect Mike Shanahan for that. He nurtured an environment that allowed us to compete, and the best player won. That's all anybody can ask for.

Super Bowl XXXII Denver Broncos vs. Green Bay Packers

Going into the game we were heavy underdogs. Green Bay had Brett Favre, Reggie White, and the NFC had won 13 straight Super Bowls. Here we were, a team that nobody thought had a chance. We felt different. We felt like we were built a little bit more like a NFC team. We had gone through enough adversity and didn't think that anybody could beat us if we played our game. That season we played Pittsburgh and Kansas City in their home stadiums and won. We felt if we could win in those two places, which were the toughest venues to play in, we could play anybody on a neutral field. We liked our chances.

Going into the game we felt confident. I knew that the game hinged on my performance. That's a lot of pressure for anyone, but I was prepared and excited for the opportunity. I felt comfortable with the game plan since we were going to run the ball 40 times. That told me a lot. When a coaching staff puts together a game plan which involves using you that much, as a competitor and as somebody who wants to be able to control the outcome of a game, you can't ask for anything better than that.

The night before the game, I slept like a baby. People ask me, "Man, weren't you nervous?" I respond, "Yeah, but I was prepared, and more excited than anything." I'd much rather go to sleep knowing we're going to run the ball 40 times than go to bed knowing we're going to throw it 50 times in a game. That would have been unsettling. I wouldn't have been able to affect the game like I wanted to.

The game starts and we are down seven-nothing very quickly. No one panicked. Everybody looked around and said, "Okay, they scored. We've got to score." We did that. We knew it was going to be a tough game. It was not going to be an easy game by any means. Our feeling was if we don't screw up, we're going to win the game.

Then I got a migraine in the first quarter. That was devastating, because I thought I had let everyone down. I thought I had let my teammates, fans, and myself down because I had to leave the game. I was sick thinking about the next day's headline of Denver losing this game and me not being able to help out. That hurt me.

I tried to get back as fast as I could. I end up coming back in the third quarter. Fortunately, I was able to come back when we were either tied or leading. I fumbled the first snap of the third quarter, which was not good.

It was a back and forth, very exciting game. I just stayed focused and tried not to think about the outcome. I was trying to think about my job and my responsibilities. I was trying to play my role as best as I could. I felt if I did that, then we had a great chance of winning the game. I tried to stay in the moment, and was ble to do that. At the end of the game I looked at the scoreboard and saw we won 31-24.

The thing that stands out to me a lot is when John Mobley knocked down a pass that Brett Favre intended for Mark Chmura. I still replay that play in my head a lot because that was the culmination, the exclamation point on a season that we had fought our asses off during. To beat Green Bay, and to upset that team was exciting. I was exhausted at the end of the game. I will always remember that final play.

Suffering From Migraines

I've had migraines since I was eight or nine years old. I remember playing football with a migraine when I had no idea that I suffered from migraines. I was not diagnosed at the time. I was so ashamed, because I couldn't explain to anybody what was going on. I felt guilty about telling somebody how I felt, because I couldn't explain it. I played in a couple of high school games with full-blown migraines with no medication whatsoever. It was probably the most difficult thing that I had ever had to do.

In college, I was diagnosed with migraines. They would come every so often, and I could take medication. The medication would at least numb the headache. The headache wouldn't be as intense.

I played a few games with migraines in the pros. Against Tampa Bay I got hit in the head by Hardy Nickerson during the first quarter. I missed the second quarter and came back out and played in the third quarter. With that history, when I got the migraine in the Super Bowl, I knew that there was a chance that I could come back. Thank God the halftime shows are super long, because it allowed the medication to kick in. I knew I was going to be able to come back.

That was the hope. My saving grace was I knew I would come back; it was just a matter of when. What would happen during the game while I was away was what I was concerned about.

When I got back, my vision was clear. It's like you have a hangover. Your head is still a little sensitive. I had no choice though; I had to play. If it was a regular season game, chances are I would have sit out. I couldn't in this case. I wouldn't have been able to forgive myself for not going back into the game, especially if we had lost the game. I was like, hey, do it now, go through the pain and suck it up. I can rest tomorrow, the next day, the next day, and a whole six months from now. Today you got to go.

John Elway Utilizing The Running Game More Later On In His Career

John Elway has never said this but I imagine behind the scenes it was tough for him to hand the ball off more because I think it's a sign that maybe he was not the same quarterback he used to be. That's tough for anybody to swallow. I would feel the same way if the roles were reversed. If we were a running team, then we get a quarterback and we start to throw it, I would feel the same way.

It wasn't like we were running the ball and we weren't successful. It wasn't like we were just running the ball a lot and he was not getting a chance to throw the ball. John still threw the ball a lot. We still had game plans where we threw a lot since we knew we couldn't run the ball against a team like we want to. It was important for John to be able to throw the ball, because we needed that to keep the opponent from putting extra defenders in the box, or doing things to slow down the running game. The balance we had in

Denver was perfect. If the defense put too many people up there in the box, we knew John was going to kill the opponent throwing the ball. I don't know if John has ever said it publicly, but I just know that if it were me and we were used to being a running team and all of a sudden we were a passing team, deep down inside it would kind of hurt. You want to be the person that the team relies on. The way I look at it is we didn't take anything from John; we added something to what he was doing which allowed us to be a better team.

Not Breaking Eric Dickerson's Single Season Rushing Yardage Record

I probably could have broken his record. I didn't care about records at that time. I only cared about one thing, and that was if we were winning games, in the playoffs, and playing for the Vince Lombardi Trophy. That's the only thing I cared about. I cared less about 2000- yard seasons and whatnot.

This shows I didn't care, because there was one against Philadelphia and one against Dallas where the coach asked me if I wanted to stay in. I got pulled at halftime against Philadelphia and early in the third period against Dallas. I think in both of those games I had over 150 yards rushing. I didn't care about the record. I just wanted to be as healthy as possible so that I could help the team win a championship. That's really all I cared about.

1999 NFL Playoffs

We felt pretty confident about Atlanta. We were probably a little bit more concerned if Minnesota had made the Super Bowl. We were watching Atlanta play against Minnesota in the NFL Championship Game as we were preparing to play the New York Jets in the AFC Championship Game. When Minnesota lost we got pretty excited in our locker room. Everybody was like, "Oh, Minnesota lost, wow."

We were thinking it's going to be an easy AFC Championship Game. Somebody forgot to tell us we had a game to play. The Jets came in and we were down 10-0 early in the third quarter. We woke up and came back and won the game.

When we got ready to play Atlanta in the Super Bowl, we felt we matched up well against them. We felt like Green Bay did the year before when they played us in the Super Bowl. Knowing how the media was pumping us up, we had to really check our way of thinking. Our thinking was we knew what happened last year when Green Bay was favored by double digits against us. Now we're being favored. We have to make sure we stay focused, and don't believe the hype. We know we're good, but we've got to make sure we don't buy into all that stuff and think that we just have to show up to win the game against Atlanta.

We played a hell of a game, so I was proud of us. We went out there and played a good game.

John Elway's Decision To Retire After Super Bowl Win Against Atlanta Falcons

Man, we tried to convince John Elway not to retire after winning the Super Bowl against Atlanta. What people don't realize is he was beat up. John missed a lot of practice time. He was constantly in rehab, icing shoulders and knees. He gave us all he could give us. We appreciate him giving us that. We were trying to do everything to convince him not to retire. I was hoping that Mike Shanahan would say, "Hey John, sit out training camp, relax, we'll see you in early September. You just play in regular season games." We needed to have him back. It's hard when someone walks out after you win two Super Bowls, and you don't really give yourself a chance to win three in a row. You've got to go for it!

We understood his decision. We didn't like it, but we had to go forward. Obviously things didn't turn out too well after that. That flame burned out real quick.

Numerous Injuries Sustained After 1998 Season
It was a constant struggle trying to fight injury. I never regained my health. It's hard to be an elite athlete when you're fighting injuries and just trying to become a healthy player, let alone a player who was trained to play on a different level. It was mentally draining, more than anything. That was rough.

Mile High Salute
The Mile High Salute started in training camping in 1997. We had lost to Jacksonville the year before in the playoffs. I was just trying to think of something where we had to have a mentality for that year. The mentality that I was looking for was that of a soldier. This was for the running backs in particular. I was saying, "Hey guys, when we're on the field we have to adopt a mentality that is nasty, that is physical; you've got determination, you've got to do all this stuff." I was thinking about who represents that. A Soldier.

Being a soldier is not like being a football player where you go play football and then you walk off the field. Soldiers go out there and they put their lives on the line. Out of respect, I thought this is what we're going to do. When we score, we're going to salute each other. That's our Mile High Salute to each other, out of respect as soldiers.

We did it in the preseason and started doing it during the season. It just took off. Everybody on the team started to do it.

Selection To Pro Football Hall Of Fame
From what everybody was saying, they thought my career was too short to make the Pro Football Hall Of Fame. Then I made the semifinalist list for the Hall Of Fame. That was the first year I actually got excited. I was thinking maybe there's a chance I make the Hall Of Fame. I made it again as a semifinalist and got excited again. I felt maybe there were people talking about me making the Hall Of Fame again.

The following years there weren't a whole lot of conversations about me making the Hall Of Fame. I'd see my name on the list, and when I would watch sports shows, people would talk about everybody else on the list except me. They might ask somebody, who on this list do you think deserves to be in the Hall Of Fame? No one would say me. Then I thought, I guess I'm not going to make it.

About year seven I really felt like, maybe this is where I'm going to be all the time. Maybe I'll just make the list of semifinalists, and that's it. Not that I was okay with it, but I was like, okay, that's where they're going to put me. You can't do anything about it. You can't go play any more, and you can't control it, so I tried not to worry about it.

Then, in 2014 they called me while I was driving with my wife and told me that I had advanced from the semifinalist list to the finalist list. I was fired up. I pulled over and told her, "You won't believe what happened." She's like, "What, what?" I said, "I just made the finalist list for the Hall Of Fame." We screamed and hugged each other on the side of the road. It was big. That kind of got me rejuvenated. That kind of got me thinking maybe there's something to it.

The following three years, it started to feel like there was more momentum behind it. More people were talking about it. When I would watch a show, I would see guys who didn't endorse me early on, change their opinions about me. It was great to see that. It was a good feeling to see people stop looking at the length of my career, and start to look at the substance of what happened.

I couldn't control whether I played seven or 20 years. The one thing I could control was the effort I gave when I played. I think people can look at that and say, "Damn, when he played, this dude gave it his all. My teammates will say, 'TD gave everything, TD played his ass off when he played.'" To me, that's the biggest compliment I can get. Knowing that I got your back, no matter what it is, I'm going to show up; I'm going to be there and showup. It was great to see the selection committee looked at that. It's a tough process, and it should be tough, because it's more rewarding when it happens.

I had so many emotions running through my head when Dave Baker, President of The Pro Football Hall Of Fame, told me I had been selected to the Hall. I was relieved, excited, and had jubilation. My mind was flipping the channel on what this all meant. I was thinking about things I wouldn't have to say anymore. I was like, thank God. I was thinking about the people that I had seen with these gold jackets on, and thinking that now I am one of them.

Photograph copyright Associated Press

www.ingramcontent.com/pod-product-compliance
Lightning Source LLC
Chambersburg PA
CBHW051900090426
42811CB00003B/409